One Man and One Woman
Marriage and Same-Sex Relations

One Man and One Woman
Marriage and Same-Sex Relations

Joel R. Beeke and Paul M. Smalley

Reformation Heritage Books
Grand Rapids, Michigan

One Man and One Woman: Marriage and Same-Sex Relations
©2016 by Joel R. Beeke and Paul M. Smalley

Reformation Heritage Books
2965 Leonard St. NE
Grand Rapids, MI 49525
616-977-0889 / Fax 616-285-3246
orders@heritagebooks.org
www.heritagebooks.org

Printed in the United States of America
16 17 18 19 20 21/10 9 8 7 6 5 4 3 2 1

ISBN: 978-1-60178-474-2 (print)
       978-1-60178-475-9 (epub)

For additional Reformed literature, both new and used, request a free book list from Reformation Heritage Books at the above regular or e-mail address.

Table of Contents

Foreword by Rosaria Butterfield vii

1. Foundations: Love, Authority, and Sexuality . . 1
2. Directions: God's Word to Ancient Israel
   about Homosexuality 27
3. Expectations: The Power of Sin and the
   Power of Christ 47
4. Conclusions: Grace and Truth 67

Bibliography of Works Cited 77

Foreword

We live in a time of radical sea change in sexual ethics. Indeed, even the very language that we use to represent people and relationships has been turned upside down. Words that used to assure stability of meaning—male, female, wife, husband—are routinely redefined by our secular culture so that they no longer mean what they describe. Our culture is more and more bold in its rejection of the Bible, casting it off as irrelevant or even dangerous. It also dismisses the sovereign power of a theistic God, the Creator of the universe and all humanity, who intervenes in the affairs of this world and sustains an intimate personal relationship with His people.

This moral revolt is breaking down our language into alphabet soup. No longer are people understood to be, ontologically, image bearers of a holy God, born male or female by design and purpose. Instead, we are told we are somewhere in the gender and sexuality continuum—LGBTQIAP—lesbian, gay, bisexual, transgender, queer, questioning, intersex, asexual, pansexual. This arbitrary alphabet is both pervasive and inaccessible; indeed, it is only discernible to a select few. What are Christian parents to do if their covenant child returns from college identifying himself under the umbrella of these letters? How can one respond to a problem that we don't understand? In times like these, the Bible's wisdom seems to operate in a parallel universe to the culture's new rules and norms, and even believers feel unmoored and without hope.

We did not arrive at this problem overnight. The 2015 Supreme Court decision in Obergefell v. Hodges that gave constitutional right to gay marriage escalated a problem that started in the garden of Eden. Because certain categories of reality depend upon exclusivity to exist, gay marriage could not add a new dimension to the integrity of biblical marriage without erupting it. Gay marriage is as much an attack on personhood as it is on marriage. Today, in this era of late modernity, the progressive nature of original sin has degenerated into a world where declaring that there are ethical and moral responsibilities and constraints to being born male and female is considered by the world to be either hate speech or mere stupidity.

We live in a time where good is called evil and evil is called good.

And sadly, shamefully, this is the world that I helped create. I lived as a lesbian and advocated for this moral revolution for ten years of my life. And only when I met the risen Lord did I see how woefully and dangerously wrong I had been.

The book you hold in your hand is a pastoral guide through the landscape and land mines of this moral revolution, with the light of the gospel leading the way. Because we are all distorted by original sin, distracted by actual sin, and manipulated by indwelling sin, we are an easily deceived people in great need of pastoral shepherding as we navigate the terms and consequences of this mutiny.

Christians who struggle with unwanted homosexual desires will find in this book loving reminders of what union with Christ promises as we fight against indwelling sin. Parents of adult children who identify as gay or lesbian will better understand how to listen to the discerning words of Scripture as they shake the gates of heaven for their children. And all Christians will be better able to understand and defend why the God who created us has exclusive claims in defining what it means to be male and female and designing biblical marriage as an ordinance of creation and therefore a glorious institution that God made for His glory and our good.

—Rosaria Butterfield

Chapter 1

Foundations: Love, Authority, and Sexuality

People are asking questions. "My friend told me she is proud to go to a church where the pastor is a lesbian. What should I say?" "Should I go to the wedding of my cousin, knowing that he is engaged to another man?" "My son feels so confused about who he is, and one of his friends is telling him that there's nothing wrong with gay relationships if you love each other. How can I give him guidance?" "Why do some churches say that the Bible is not against homosexuality? What does the Bible really say about it?"

Few subjects stir up as much controversy today among professing Christians as that of sexual relationships between people of the same gender. For nearly two thousand years, churches uniformly opposed same-sex sexual activity as sinful. That unity has now been shattered. In the last few decades, some denominations have welcomed people practicing same-sex erotic activity into membership and even ordained ministry. Many Reformed and Evangelical writers still teach that homosexuality is a violation of the laws of God, a sin which Christ must forgive and break its ruling power if we are to count ourselves as Christians.[1] However, an increasing number of people and churches say that one can practice homosexuality and be a Christian.[2] Both positions claim

---

1. This is the historic position of the Christian church. Some recent books supporting it include Sam Allberry, *Is God Anti-gay? And Other Questions about Homosexuality, the Bible and Same-Sex Attraction* (Epsom, Surrey, U.K.: The Good Book Company, 2013); Michael L. Brown, *Can You Be Gay and Christian? Responding with Love and Truth to Questions about Homosexuality* (Lake Mary, Fl.: Charisma House, 2014); Rosaria Champagne Butterfield, *Openness Unhindered: Further Thoughts of an Unlikely Convert on Sexual Identity and Union with Christ* (Pittsburgh: Crown and Covenant, 2015); Mark Christopher, *Same-sex Marriage: Is It Really the Same?* (Leominster, U.K.: Day One, 2009); Kevin DeYoung, *What Does the Bible Really Teach about Homosexuality?* (Wheaton, Ill.: Crossway, 2015); Robert A. J. Gagnon, *The Bible and Homosexual Practice: Texts and Hermeneutics* (Nashville: Abingdon Press, 2001); R. Albert Mohler Jr., ed., *God and the Gay Christian? A Response to Matthew Vines* (Louisville, Ky.: SBTS Press, 2014), free ebook accessed August 4, 2015, available from http://sbts.me/ebook, henceforth cited as *Response to Matthew Vines*; Synod of the Reformed Presbyterian Church in North America (RPCNA), *The Gospel and Sexual Orientation*, ed. Michael Lefebvre (Pittsburgh: Crown and Covenant, 2012); James R. White and Jeffrey D. Niell, *The Same Sex Controversy* (Bloomington, Minn.: Bethany House, 2002); Donald J. Wold, *Out of Order: Homosexuality in the Bible and the Ancient Near East* (Grand Rapids: Baker, 1998).

2. Tom Horner, *Jonathan Loved David: Homosexuality in Biblical Times* (Philadelphia: Westminster Press, 1978); David G.

the moral high ground. No doubt many outsiders find the debate confusing, and ask, "What do Christians believe about homosexuality?"[3]

Myers and Letha Dawson Scanzoni, *What God Has Joined Together? A Christian Case for Gay Marriage* (New York: Harper Collins, 2005); Pim Pronk, *Against Nature? Types of Moral Argumentation Regarding Homosexuality*, trans. John Vriend (Grand Rapids: Eerdmans, 1993); Letha Dawson Scanzoni and Virginia Ramey Mollenkott, *Is the Homosexual My Neighbor? A Positive Christian Response*, rev. ed. (New York: HarperCollins, 1994); Dan. O. Via and Robert A. J. Gagnon, *Homosexuality and the Bible: Two Views* (Minneapolis: Augsburg Fortress, 2003); Matthew Vines, *God and the Gay Christian: The Biblical Case in Support of Same-Sex Relationships* (Colorado Springs: Convergent Books, 2014).

3. Even the terminology can be confusing. Writers of previous eras spoke of male-to-male sex as *sodomy*, an allusion to the ancient city of Sodom. The word *homosexuality* was not coined until the late nineteenth century. The media currently prefers to use the words *gay* and *lesbian*. See *The Associate Press Stylebook and Briefing on Media Law, 2013* (New York: Basic Books, 2013), 114. Others use the acronym *LGBT* to include bisexual and transgender, the latter referring to persons identifying themselves as a different gender than that of their biological birth. Some find even this terminology an oversimplification of queer sexuality, too confining, or failing to account for fluid and changing desires. The phrase *same-sex attraction* (SSA) is used as well, though this may fail to distinguish between sexual attraction and emotional attraction. In this book, we will generally use the adjective *homosexual* (*homo* being from the Greek word for "same," not the Latin word for "man") since it encompasses both male-to-male and female-to-female sexuality, although with the caveat that we do not

In this book, we will set forth the basic teachings of the Holy Scriptures on homosexual desires and acts, and respond to arguments often used by those of differing viewpoints. In a short work such as this, we cannot address all practical questions about how to love and serve people with homosexual inclinations, or how to live as Christians in a cultural and political environment hostile to the Word of God. However, we do intend this short book to be very practical, a tool to equip the people of God to speak the truth in love.

On what basis do we make decisions regarding sex? What gives anyone the right to make moral pronouncements about such a personal matter? How do we know what gender and marriage mean?

The Law of Love and the Teachings of the Bible

The questions raised by homosexuality are deeply personal, for the most important factors in this controversy are not civil laws and policies, but human persons whom God calls into right relationship with Him through the gospel of Jesus Christ. Sometimes they are persons whom we know, persons close to us. Always they are persons whom God calls us to

---

endorse the idea of an immutable sexual orientation sometimes implied in the term.

love: "Thou shalt love thy neighbour as thyself" (Lev. 19:18), a command second in importance only to "thou shalt love the Lord thy God with all thy heart" (Matt. 22:37–39).

Some people would say that the discussion need go no further than, "Love thy neighbor." There is no absolute law, they say, except the law of love. They dismiss or reinterpret the teachings of the Bible because they claim that the rejection of homosexuality causes great harm to people inclined to it.[4] If labeling homosexuality as sin produces bad results for people, then the label must be wrong.[5] One man wrote, "Any interpretation that hurts people, oppresses people, or destroys people cannot be the right interpretation."[6] The love of God, we are told, requires the church to accept unconditionally those who practice homosexuality.

Cruel words spoken and violent actions done by professing Christians have hurt people deeply. Slander and murder are forbidden by the Bible. We hear

---

4. Scanzoni and Mollenkott, *Is the Homosexual My Neighbor*, 1–3, 6, 28–29, 43, 46, 51–52. Vines, *God and the Gay Christian*, 12, 18–19, 25, 29–30, 50, 95–96, 129, 156–58, 165–67, 169–72.

5. Vines, *God and the Gay Christian*, 14, 129. On Vines's abuse of Christ's metaphor of bearing good fruit, see Denny Burk, "Suppressing the Truth in Unrighteousness: Matthew Vines' Take on the New Testament," in *Response to Matthew Vines*, 55.

6. Dale Martin, cited in Brown, *Can You Be Gay and Christian?*, 201.

the pain in the words of one secret lesbian, "If the people in my church really believed that gay people could be transformed by Christ, they wouldn't talk about us or pray about us in the hateful way that they do."[7] Christians must repent of their failure to be like Christ in His love for sinners, and of their own failure to walk in humility, knowing that they too are sinners.

However, the Scriptures also teach that unrepentant homosexuality harms people. It degrades them in this present life (Rom. 1:27) and excludes them from the kingdom of God forever (1 Cor. 6:9–10). Love is patient and kind, yet love does not rejoice in sin but rejoices in the truth (1 Cor. 13:4, 6). Therefore, in love we must speak the truth and call people to repent of their sins—even as we repent of ours (Eph. 4:15; Matt. 4:17; 7:5).

To say that the only law is the law of love is not obedience to God's Word, but situational ethics, a form of moral relativism that rejects the teachings of the Bible in order to follow our feelings. Christ did not say, "Just love one another, and don't worry about the rest of the Bible," but gave a host of specific commands and teachings. How can we know what hurts or heals, what oppresses or liberates, and what

---

7. Anonymous, quoted in Rosaria Champagne Butterfield, *The Secret Thoughts of an Unlikely Convert: An English Professor's Journey into Christian Faith*, expanded ed. (Pittsburgh: Crown and Covenant, 2015), 25.

destroys or saves people, apart from God's Word? Christ did not come to abolish God's laws, but to fulfill them (Matt. 5:17). He said, "If ye love me, keep my commandments" (John 14:15). God's laws teach us what love means: "By this we know that we love the children of God, when we love God, and keep his commandments" (1 John 5:2). Therefore, we must love one another, and learn from the Scriptures what God commands.

Sexual Orientation and the Authority and Sufficiency of the Holy Scriptures

When we come to a question like this, we need more than human authority to render a verdict. In this controversy, people often attempt to make a case based on the opinions of experts, whether psychologists, theologians, biologists, sociologists, or lawyers. As informative as such writers may be, they are mere men and women, and often err and contradict each other. Christians have long affirmed that "God alone is Lord of the conscience."[8] Therefore, only the Word

---

8. Westminster Confession of Faith (20.2), in *Reformed Confessions of the Sixteenth and Seventeenth Centuries in English Translation: Volume 4, 1600–1693*, comp. James T. Dennison (Grand Rapids: Reformation Heritage Books, 2014), 257. The London Baptist Confession of 1677/1689 (21.2) makes the same statement (4:557).

of God can determine our standards and beliefs about what pleases Him.

The Bible of the Old and New Testament is the written word of God. Paul wrote in 2 Timothy 3:16–17, "All scripture is given by inspiration of God, and is profitable for doctrine, for reproof, for correction, for instruction in righteousness: that the man of God may be perfect, throughly furnished unto all good works."

As we will see in the following pages, the Bible does speak to homosexuality, and it unequivocally and repeatedly condemns it as a sin from which people must be saved by Christ. There is not a single example of a positive commendation of homosexuality in Scripture. This is acknowledged even by many who desire to promote same-sex relationships.[9]

Given the clear statements in the Scriptures against homosexuality, how can a person claim to be a Christian and yet justify homosexuality? The argument often made is that *the Scriptures do not speak*

---

9. "Wherever homosexual intercourse is mentioned in Scripture, it is condemned." Pronk, *Against Nature*, 279. Via writes, "The biblical texts that deal specifically with homosexual practice condemn it unconditionally." Via and Gagnon, *Homosexuality and the Bible: Two Views*, 93. See also Luke Timothy Johnson and Diarmaid MacCulloch, cited in DeYoung, *What Does the Bible Really Teach about Homosexuality?*, 132.

to the modern understanding of a person's sexual orientation.[10]

In response, we must first ask what they mean by "sexual orientation." According to the American Psychological Association, "Sexual orientation refers to an enduring pattern of emotional, romantic, and/or sexual attractions to men, women, or both sexes."[11] Thus orientation is a remarkably broad and indefinite concept based upon a person's experience of social and sexual desires.[12] The Scriptures speak very positively of emotional connections and friendships between people of the same sex. However, with regard to sexual desires, though the Bible does not use the term *orientation*, it speaks of male sexual desire toward males and female sexual desire for females, and condemns such desires (Rom. 1:26–27). Thus Scripture does address the orientation of a per-

---

10. Hendrik Hart, foreword to Pronk, *Against Nature*, xi; Vines, *God and the Gay Christian*, 21–41, 129. Mohler says of Vines, "His main argument is that the Bible simply has no category of sexual orientation." Mohler, "God, the Gospel and the Gay Challenge: A Response to Matthew Vines," in *Response to Matthew Vines*, 14.

11. American Psychological Association, *Answers to Your Questions: For a Better Understanding of Sexual Orientation and Homosexuality* (Washington, DC: American Psychological Association, 2008), 1, accessed August 4, 2015, https://www.apa.org /topics/lgbt/orientation.pdf.

12. Mohler, "God, the Gospel and the Gay Challenge," in *Response to Matthew Vines*, 18.

son's sexual attractions. It is not true to say that the Bible has a hole in it, and we must fill the hole with man's wisdom about sexual orientation.

The modern concept of sexual orientation, however, goes beyond a description of our desires; it seeks to set a new definition of identity and personhood. The Word of God teaches that our identity is found in being created in the image of God (Gen. 1:26). Therefore, our lives are defined by how we relate to God and His will. In the modern, secular perspective, our identity as human persons is found in our feelings and emotional experiences.[13] This perspective grows out of the philosophical movement known as Romanticism. Secular psychologists from Freud onward have especially focused our identity on our *sexual* feelings.[14] This fundamental shift in how we define our identity sets the stage for people to claim a "homosexual sexual orientation" as their basic identity. Thus any attack on the goodness of homosexuality is an

---

13. This expresses one side of our modern dualism in the secular hybrid of the philosophies of the Enlightenment and Romanticism. The modern perspective divides truth into two separate categories: that which is scientific, empirical, physical, and deterministic; versus that which is personal, emotional, spiritual, and free. Nancy R. Pearcey, *Total Truth: Liberating Christianity from Its Cultural Captivity* (Wheaton, Ill.: Crossway, 2004), 101–109. Thus personal matters are held to be entirely subjective, which is a rejection of the authority of God.

14. Butterfield, *Openness Unhindered*, 94–95.

attack on their persons. We must reject this distorted sense of identity. Our changing emotions and experiences cannot define us. God is the Creator and Lord of all. He made us by His word, and He continues to define us by His word. The most basic question about our identity is not, "How do I feel?" but "How am I representing God as His living image?"

This objection also misunderstands the Bible's teaching on sin. Not all sin is a direct act of the will or conscious choice. As the last of the Ten Commandments shows, sin also includes evil desires (Ex. 20:17). Since the fall of mankind from our original state of righteousness, the very mindset of the human race is fundamentally hostile to God, our desires have become corrupt lusts, and our hearts evil (Gen. 3:6; 6:5; 8:17; Jer. 17:9; Rom. 3:10–12; 8:7–8; Eph. 2:3). Though believers in Christ are so changed by God's Spirit as to "delight in the law of God after the inward man," they still find "evil is present" in themselves when they choose to do good (Rom. 7:21–22). The Bible calls this indwelling evil "sin" (Rom. 7:20). Therefore, part of our sinfulness is our corrupt desires that lead to sinful choices and actions.[15] To say that

---

15. This view of sin is one of the distinguishing characteristics of the Reformation faith (following Augustine) as distinct from Roman Catholicism, which sees corrupt desires as disordered but not sinful. Denny Burk, "Is Homosexual Orientation Sin?" *Journal of the Evangelical Theological Society* 58, no. 1 (2015): 97–99.

homosexuality is deeply rooted in a person through tenacious desires does not prove it to be right; many of our desires are stubbornly corrupted by sin. If a person's desires are oriented toward something forbidden by God's Word, then that orientation is sinful. Therefore, while there is nothing wrong with emotional attachments and social desires toward people of the same gender, a *sexual* attraction towards a person of the same sex is sinful.

Someone might object, however, that the biblical writers were ignorant of what modern science has shown, namely, that biology determines sexual orientation through brain structure, hormones, and/or genetics. This objection misrepresents the findings of science.[16] Both professional psychologists and psychiatrists acknowledge that, while people often do not consciously choose their desires, the cause of such desires cannot be simplistically attributed to biology. They acknowledge that we do not understand how biology and personal experiences shape sexual desire.[17] If sexuality were determined simply

---

16. Christopher, *Same-sex Marriage*, 29–32.

17. "There is no consensus among scientists about the exact reasons that an individual develops a heterosexual, bisexual, gay, or lesbian orientation…. Many think that nature and nurture both play complex roles; most people experience little or no sense of choice about their sexual orientation." American Psychological Association, *Answers to Your Questions: For a*

by genetics, then in a pair of identical twins, both twins would have the same sexual inclinations—but this is often not the case.[18]

Even if certain biological factors do tend to lead to homosexual inclinations, this does not prove such inclinations to be innocent. The Bible teaches that original sin has brought disorder to man's body and soul so that even our bodies must be brought into submission and cleansed from defilement.[19] If it could be proven that some people have a genetic tendency towards becoming rapists, we would certainly not justify sexual violence on that basis.

Better Understanding of Sexual Orientation and Homosexuality, 2. "The American Psychiatric Association believes that the causes of sexual orientation (whether homosexual or heterosexual) are not known at this time and likely are multifactorial including biological and behavioral roots which may vary between different individuals and may even vary over time." American Psychiatric Association, "Position Statement on Issues Related to Homosexuality" (2013), accessed August 5, 2015, http://www.psychiatry .org/File%20Library/Learn/Archives/Position-2013-Homosexuality.pdf.

18. "Sexual orientation is not an immutable part of our biology.... If it were, the concordance rate would not be so low between identical twins (i.e., both twins would always have the same sexual orientation, which is not the case)." DeYoung, What Does the Bible Really Teach about Homosexuality, 112. See Gagnon, The Bible and Homosexual Practice, 403–406.

19. Rom. 6:19; 7:24; 8:10, 13; 1 Cor. 9:27; 2 Cor. 7:1. See RPCNA, Gospel and Sexual Orientation, 14.

The objector might reply that, whatever the cause, many people have an inherent homosexual orientation which does not and cannot change. This is a popular claim, but it too is dubious. There are psychologists calling for a recognition of "sexual fluidity" in both men and women, that is, that desires are not immutable, but change with time and relationships.[20] A significant number of those who self-identify as "homosexuals" experience some sexual desires towards people of the opposite gender.[21] Some people inclined towards homosexuality report success after seeking to reduce same-sex desires and increase

---

20. Lisa M. Diamond, *Sexual Fluidity: Understanding Women's Love and Desire* (Cambridge: Mass.: Harvard University Press, 2009); "Just How Different are Female and Male Sexual Orientation?" video lecture, October 17, 2013, *Cornell University*, accessed August 7, 2015, http://www.cornell.edu/video/lisa -diamond-on-sexual-fluidity-of-men-and-women. She argues for "fluidity as a general feature of sexuality" for males and females of all sexual inclinations (37:38 in video). Diamond is a feminist and lesbian psychology professor at the University of Utah. See also Joe Kort, "Going with the Flow: Male and Female Sexual Fluidity," *Huffington Post: Gay Voices*, updated 4/10/2015, accessed August 7, 2015, http://www.huffingtonpost.com/joe -kort-phd/going-with-the-flow-male-_b_6642504.html. Note that Kort's blog post contains some offensive language. Butterfield writes, "No one in the LGBT community from which I emerged would have ever claimed to have been 'born this way.' We believed that sexuality was fluid." Butterfield, *Openness Unhindered*, 108.

21. Diamond, "Just How Different are Female and Male Sexual Orientation?" video lecture.

opposite-sex desires.[22] Most significantly, the Bible teaches that the Holy Spirit does change people who formerly delighted and engaged in same-sex erotic activity and gives them a new identity and a new way of life in Jesus Christ (1 Cor. 6:9–11). Again, God has spoken on this issue, and people once given over to homosexual activity can repent of this sin and be delivered from it.

This objection is also falsified by history. Rather than driving a wedge between the Bible and the modern world, we should recognize that we live in a situation well understood in the ancient world. Greco-Roman culture considered it acceptable for a man to engage in sexual activity in many different directions over the same time period or variously at different times. Thus one man might have sex with his wife, make use of female prostitutes, have a sexual relationship with another man, engage in pederasty or a socially approved sexual relationship with a teenaged boy, and commit adultery with non-prostitute women other than his wife. Though different men may have had different inclinations at various times, the culture did not have a binary concept of

---

22. Gagnon, *The Bible and Homosexual Practice*, 418–29; Stanton L. Jones and Mark A. Yarhouse, *Ex-Gays? A Longitudinal Study of Religiously Mediated Change in Sexual Orientation* (Downers Grove, Ill.: IVP Academic, 2007), 325.

definitive homosexual versus heterosexual orientations.[23] Nor is such the concept taught in the Holy Scriptures.

Another, similar objection is that the apostle Paul did not understand the possibility of a positive, affectionate sexual relationship between men, and therefore wrote only against abusive or promiscuous relationships.[24] However, it is not true to say that people in Greco-Roman culture were ignorant of the full range of sexual relationships that we know of today.[25] Vines errs when he writes that "same-sex relations… were approved only when a man dominated someone of a lower social status."[26] Though there certainly were such oppressive relationships, especially with

---

23. William L. Petersen, "Can ΑΡΣΕΝΟΚΟΙΤΑΙ Be Translated by 'Homosexuals'?" *Vigiliae Christianae* 40, no. 2 (June 1986): 188; Vines, *God and the Gay Christian*, 31–36.

24. "In the few places where same-sex sexual acts are mentioned in Scripture, the context suggests idolatry, violent rape, lust, exploitation, or promiscuity. Nothing is said about homosexual orientation as understood through modern science, nor is anything said about the loving relationship of two same-sex persons who have covenanted to be life partners." Myers and Scanzoni, *What God Has Joined Together*, 84–85.

25. DeYoung, *What Does the Bible Say about Homosexuality?*, 83–86. He cites the findings of scholars such as Thomas Hubbard (non-Christian), William Loader (proponent of same-sex marriage), Bernadette Brooten (lesbian), N. T. Wright (Anglican bishop), and Louis Crompton (gay).

26. Vines, *God and the Gay Christian*, 37.

slaves, there were also examples of male lovers both of whom were regarded as noble, such as the Greek heroes Harmodius and Aristogeiton, and according to some ancient interpretations, Achilles and Patroclus. In Plato's *Symposium*, Pausanius and Agathon shared a sexual relationship as adults, and Pausanius speaks of men entering into sexual relationships with youths that would extend into a lifetime of love.[27] The ancient world did have a concept of two men in a so-called "positive, committed relationship."

Therefore, the attempt to sideline biblical teaching as irrelevant to same-sex orientation fails. Biblical writers knew of such relationships, and included them when they wrote against homosexuality.

Christians must not embrace a view of the Bible as insufficient to guide our faith and obedience. As we saw, in 2 Timothy 3:16–17, Paul wrote that God gave us the Bible to make His servants "perfect, throughly furnished," that is, "completely equipped" for every good work, including the works of moral reproof and direction. Therefore, the Bible is sufficient for our moral instruction, and to say that it does not give us competent instruction on homosexuality is to deny the wisdom of the God who inspired it. This is not a new issue. Shall we believe that a loving God left

27. Plato, *Symposium*, 181d. See Gagnon, *The Bible and Homosexual Practice*, 351–52.

his people for thousands of years with an incomplete view of their sexuality?

If the biblical writers were silent on such an important matter concerning our sexuality, then we would have to ask, "What else does the Bible not know about what it means to be human?" In other words, as Al Mohler writes, it would imply that "the Bible simply cannot be trusted to understand what it means to be human, to reveal what God intends for us sexually, or to define sin in any coherent manner."[28] This amounts to allowing our feelings and experience to dictate our beliefs and interpretation of the Bible, instead of submitting to God to direct our beliefs and interpret our experiences through His Word.[29]

The Bible does give holistic instruction on sexuality, including homosexuality, and we must hear what it says. Furthermore, the conclusions of the social sciences are not neutral, objective facts, but

28. R. Albert Mohler Jr., "God, the Gospel and the Gay Challenge," in *Response to Matthew Vines*, 19.

29. "When he begins his book, Vines argues that experience should not drive our interpretation of the Bible. But it is his experience of what he calls a gay sexual orientation that drives every word of this book. It is this experiential issue that drives him to relativize text after text and to argue that the Bible doesn't speak directly to his sexual identity at all, since the inspired human authors of Scripture were ignorant of the modern gay experience." Mohler, "God, the Gospel and the Gay Challenge," in *Response to Matthew Vines*, 18.

the writings of people profoundly influenced by the spirit of the age. Whenever the word of man contradicts the Word of God, we must obey God.

Gender, Sexuality, and Marriage in God's Created Order

In order to understand the Bible's teaching on homosexuality, we must step back and consider what the Scriptures say about mankind and sexual relationships. God laid the foundations of these truths in the book of Genesis, which contains an historical account of mankind's origin. The first chapters of the book of Genesis teach us several key facts about the human race.

1. God created man *in the image of God* (Gen 1:27). People are not animals (Gen. 1:24–25), but God's special creations designed to reflect His character as they rule over the world (Gen. 1:26, 28). This teaches us that though mankind has fallen into misery by our sin (Genesis 3), every human life is precious (Gen. 9:6), and every human being should be treated with basic respect (James 3:9). God created the human race for His glory, and we have a high and noble calling (Isa. 43:7).

Therefore, we should not act like animals (though our bodies share similarities with some animals), or try to justify our behavior by comparing it to the behavior of animals. Our lives have a deeper meaning than our physical desires. We are spiritual beings who exist for God. We have souls. We are responsible persons made for His glory, and are accountable to our Creator. This also implies that we must treat all people with honor and dignity (1 Peter 2:17).

2. God created man *in two distinct genders*: "male and female created he them" (Gen. 1:27). God created the man first out of the earth and gave him God's law to be the leader that she needs (Gen. 2:9, 15–17; Eph. 5:23; 2 Tim. 2:13–14), and then created the woman out of the man as a "help meet for him," the helper that he needs who shares the same human nature (Gen. 2:18, 21–23). Both had the dignity and authority to rule over God's world, but were distinct from each other as male and female (Gen. 1:27–28).

This teaches us that gender is not merely a personal mindset or a social construct, but an aspect of God's fixed order in creation. The genders of the first man and woman were set when God first created them on the sixth day, and the gender of each of their offspring is set at conception.[30] The words translated

---

30. We recognize that some people are born with a mixture of male and female genitalia (*intersex* persons). However this is a rare biological abnormality resulting from the fall, and most

"male" and "female" reflect categories applicable to animals as well as humans,[31] implying that the gender of each person corresponds to his or her physical sex.[32] Both men and women share the image of God, but God designed them to function in different ways for His glory. It is very good for a man to be a man, and very good for a woman to be a woman (Gen. 1:31). They should not try to erase their differences or construct a genderless society, but to live as equal but different persons, a difference visible even in their clothing and hairstyles (Deut. 22:5; 1 Cor. 11:14–16).[33]

---

intersex individuals identify as a man or woman. This condition is distinct from homosexuality and transgenderism.

31. Gen. 6:19; 7:3, 9, 16.

32. It is not helpful to assign a person a gender identity distinct from genitalia and based upon brain biology or some personality tendencies more commonly found in the opposite sex. Jacob and Esau were quite different, but both equally male. RPCNA, *Gospel and Sexual Orientation*, 23–28.

33. Vines writes, "Adam and Eve were right for each other, not because they were different, but because they were alike." Vines, *God and the Gay Christian*, 46. On the contrary, Gen. 1–2 teaches the complementarity of the two genders both because they are alike (man created in God's image) *and different* (male and female). See Raymond C. Ortlund, Jr., "Male-Female Equality and Male Headship: Genesis 1–3," in *Recovering Biblical Manhood and Womanhood: A Response to Evangelical Feminism*, ed. John Piper and Wayne Grudem (Wheaton, Ill.: Crossway Books, 1991), 95–112. Vines refuses to recognize that both the sameness and differentiation of Adam and Eve made their union

At this point the Scriptures confront *transgender-ism*, the personal assumption of a different gender identity than one's biological sex at birth. Transgenderism is not identical to homosexuality, and is commonly treated as a distinct matter. Katy Steinmetz writes, "There is no concrete correlation between a person's gender identity and sexual interests; a heterosexual woman, for instance, might start living as a man and still be attracted to men."[34] Some would go so far as to remove any fixed sense of gender in our culture and replace it with an infinite variety of identities or an "omnigender."[35] This is rebellion against the order established by the good Creator of all things.

In today's popular rhetoric, gender is a social construct, whereas sexual orientation is an unchangeable identity. The Bible takes the exact opposite approach. The idea of sexual orientation, so often implied in the nouns homosexual and heterosexual,

---

good. This is part of his overall strategy to appeal to evangelical egalitarians to take the next logical step: if the two genders are not distinct and complementary, then they can be interchanged in sexual relations. See Mohler, "God, the Gospel and the Gay Challenge," in *Response to Matthew Vines*, 19–21.

34. Cited in R. Albert Mohler, Jr., *We Cannot Be Silent: Speaking Truth to a Culture Redefining Sex, Marriage, and the Very Meaning of Right and Wrong* (Nashville: Thomas Nelson, 2015), 68.

35. Virginia R. Mollenkott, *Omnigender: A Trans-Religious Approach* (Cleveland: Pilgrim Press, 2001). See the discussion in Mohler, *We Cannot Be Silent*, 72.

is "nothing more than a fragile social construct, and one constructed terribly recently," as Michael Hannon writes.[36] Our identity was set by our Creator when He made us in His image in two distinct genders. Mohler says, "The binary system of gender is grounded in a biological reality and is not socially constructed.... We affirm that biological sex is a gift from God to every individual and to the human community to which that individual belongs."[37]

3. God united one man and one woman *in marriage to produce children.* God said to them, "Be fruitful, and multiply" (Gen. 1:28). He oriented their sexuality towards each other in a lasting sexual bond. Through the creation of the first man and woman, God revealed His purpose for marriage: "Therefore shall a man leave his father and his mother, and shall cleave unto his wife: and they shall be one flesh" (Gen. 2:24). The Lord Jesus Christ quoted this statement as the word of the Creator, and taught us to build our view of marriage upon it (Matt. 19:4–6).

Since God provided an authoritative pattern for the marital, sexual relation, we are not free to create our own forms of sexuality according to our desires

---

36. Michael W. Hannon, "Against Heterosexuality: The Idea of Sexual Orientation Is Artificial and Inhibits Christian Witness," *First Things,* no. 241 (March 2014): 28.

37. Mohler, *We Cannot Be Silent,* 80.

or imagination. God's answer for mankind's sexual needs is: "let every man have his own wife, and let every woman have her own husband" (1 Cor. 7:2). Marriage was not invented by man, and man has no right to define marriage as he pleases. Marriage is God's gift for the mutual help and companionship of one man and one woman. Its link to bearing children shows that one purpose of marriage is the bringing of children into the world, a purpose that requires the participation of a man and a woman (Gen. 1:27–28; 4:1, 25).

4. Although God created human gender, sexuality, and marriage in perfect goodness (Gen. 1:31), mankind quickly *fell from this happy state into sin and misery* by disobeying God's command. Sin entered the world, not just bad decisions but a distortion of human thinking and desires (Gen. 3:6). The verdict of God over the whole human race, apart from those under God's saving grace, is that every purpose of the thoughts of our hearts is "only evil continually," even from our childhood (Gen. 6:5; 8:21).

Therefore, we cannot build our sense of right and wrong about sexuality (or anything else) upon our own thoughts and feelings. Mankind is corrupted and darkened by sin, with the result that people may commit sexual sin with little or no remorse (Eph. 4:17–19). We turn things upside-down, provoking

God to exclaim, "Woe unto them that call evil good, and good evil; that put darkness for light, and light for darkness; that put bitter for sweet, and sweet for bitter!" (Isa. 5:20). Our only hope to know the truth is the Word and Spirit of God.

The very words homosexual and heterosexual arose from an attempt to define people according to their sexual desires. This distorts our identity. While our sexual desires are an important aspect of who we are, they are far from the core of our identity. Rosaria Butterfield writes, "If I self-define as heterosexual or homosexual…everything, including nonsexual affection, is subsumed by this new humanity of sexuality."[38] We must resist the attempt to make our feelings into our identity, and instead learn our identity from our Creator. Rather than saying, "I am a homosexual," or "I am a heterosexual," we should say, "I am a man or woman created in the image of God for His glory, but fallen into sin." The Bible's call to repentance is not a call to change from one sexual orientation to another. Butterfield says, "You cannot repent of sexual orientation, since sexual orientation is an artificial category built on a faulty premise."[39] The call to repentance is a call to reject the lie that our sexual desires define us, and to submit to the

---

38. Butterfield, *Openness Unhindered*, 98.
39. Butterfield, *Openness Unhindered*, 107.

authority of God's Word in order to learn who we are and what we must become.

Therefore, the Bible offers us foundations on which to build a true and realistic view of human sexuality. Rather than simplistically say, "All we need is love," we have recourse to God's detailed instructions throughout Scripture. The Bible does address homosexuality, and it does so in the context of a view of marriage as the union of two divinely created genders, man and woman.

Chapter 2

Directions: God's Word to Ancient Israel about Homosexuality

What does the Old Testament of the Bible teach us specifically about same-sex activity? Is modern homosexuality condemned by God's judgment on Sodom? Why is the law to ancient Israel relevant to us today?

The Wicked and Tragic City of Sodom

The most well-known historical references to homosexuality in Scripture are those of Sodom, a city noted for its great wickedness (Gen. 13:13; 18:20). Though Abraham rescued its people in the process of saving his nephew Lot from an invading army, Abraham refused to have any dealings with the king of Sodom (Gen. 14:21–23). The Lord did not find ten righteous people there, and therefore destroyed the city in a spectacular outpouring of fire and brimstone visible for miles around (Gen. 18:32; 19:24–29).

Genesis gives two indications of the wickedness that provoked this act of judgment. First, there was *grave injustice.* The Lord said the "cry" of the city has risen up to Him (Gen. 18:20–21; 19:13). The Hebrew root behind "cry" refers to shriek or scream, generally a call for help and in many cases with the implication of a people oppressed and crying for justice.[1] The prophet Ezekiel confirmed that the rich and power-ful people in Sodom crushed the poor: "Behold, this was the iniquity of thy sister Sodom, pride, fulness of bread, and abundance of idleness was in her and in her daughters, neither did she strengthen the hand of the poor and needy. And they were haughty, and committed abomination before me: therefore I took them away as I saw good" (Ezek. 16:49–50). The first sin of Sodom was *pride,* an arrogance that moves us to act as if we were independent from God and to use people for our own pleasure and glory.

Second, there was *sexual perversion* in Sodom. When two angels appearing as men came to town and stayed with Lot, all the men of Sodom, "both old and young" surrounded Lot's house and demanded, "Where are the men which came in to thee this

---

1. See the use of צעק and its cognates in contexts of abuse and injustice in Gen. 4:10; Ex. 3:7, 9; 5:15; 22:23, 27; Num. 20:16; Deut. 22:24, 27; 26:7; Job 34:28. Thus Victor P. Hamilton, *The Book of Genesis, Chapters 18–50,* New International Commentary on the Old Testament (Grand Rapids: Eerdmans, 1995), 20–21.

night? Bring them out unto us, that we may know them" (Gen. 19:4–5). This was no innocent attempt to welcome the newcomers; Lot calls it a wicked act (v. 7). The Hebrew word "know" is used as a euphemism for sexual intercourse.[2] Lot's reference to "two daughters which have not known a man," that is, who were sexual virgins (v. 8), confirms that "know" in this context is sexual.[3]

Some may object that the men of Sodom sought to rape the visitors, and therefore their sin was not homosexual activity, but the violent abuse of power.[4] Certainly rape was in view here, perhaps as an example of their proud oppression of people. However, the Genesis text has strongly sexual overtones. Later writers saw the sin of Sodom as sexual perversion. Ezekiel 16:50 notes that in addition to their

---

2. Gen. 4:1, 17, 25; 19:8; 24:16; 38:26; Num. 31:17, 18, 35; Judg. 19:25; 1 Sam. 1:19; 1 Kings 1:4. The Septuagint also translates "know" with a Greek word (συγγενώμεθα) used sexually in the Scriptures (Gen. 39:10) and outside them. Wold, *Out of Order*, 82, 86–87.

3. "When Lot responds by offering his daughters 'who have never known a man' (v. 8), it becomes clear that the issue is intercourse and not friendship." Hamilton, *Genesis, Chapters 18–50*, 34. Know (ידע) "must be here intended to mean sexual intimacy, and this is recognized by all the major commentators." Gordon Wenham, *Genesis 16–50*, Word Biblical Commentary (Nashville: Thomas Nelson, 1994), 55.

4. Myers and Scanzoni, *What God Has Joined Together?*, 86–88.

proud oppression of others, the people of Sodom were guilty of "abomination." Ezekiel did not explain what abomination he had in mind, but the word is closely associated with the metaphor of sexual sin in that chapter.[5] Ezekiel makes much use of the book of Leviticus, and in Leviticus the only sin specifically named an abomination is male-with-male sex, as we will see.[6] So it may be that the abomination of Ezekiel 16:50 is Sodom's homosexual sin. Jewish writings outside of the Bible from the second century BC such as Jubilees and the Testaments of the Twelve Patriarchs also identified sexual sin as one of the great offenses of Sodom.[7]

---

5. Ezek. 16:22, 36. Ezekiel used sexual sin as a vivid picture of idolatry and infidelity to the Lord.

6. James M. Hamilton Jr., "How to Condone What the Bible Condemns: Matthew Vine's Take on the Old Testament," in *Response to Matthew Vines*, 35. "Ezekiel displays an affinity in thought and in expression with [the holiness code in Lev. 17–26] which he has with no other portion of the Pentateuch, not even with Deuteronomy." Lewis B. Paton, "The Holiness-Code and Ezekiel," *Presbyterian and Reformed Review* 7, no. 25 (January 1896): 99.

7. Jubilees 16:5–6; Testament of Levi 14:6; Testament of Benjamin 9:1; Testament of Naphtali 3:4, quoted in Gagnon, *The Bible and Homosexual Practice*, 88n121. In the first century BC, Philo wrote of Sodom, "those were men who lusted after one another, doing unseemly things, and not regarding or respecting their common nature...and so, by degrees, the men became accustomed to be treated like women." *De Abrahamo*, 136–37, cited in

It has been argued that Christ did not view Sodom's sin as a matter of sexuality but a gross violation of the requirements of hospitality to strangers.[8] In reality, the Lord Jesus did not specify the sin of Sodom, but only held it up as an example of divine judgment, warning that those cities in Galilee that rejected the gospel would suffer a worse fate (Matt. 10:14–15; 11:23–24).[9] We do note, however, that Christ warned that self-righteous religious people will fall under a more severe punishment on judgment day than the Sodomites.

Jude offers divinely inspired New Testament commentary on Sodom that condemns their sexual perversion: "Even as Sodom and Gomorrha, and the cities about them in like manner, giving themselves over to fornication, and going after strange flesh, are set forth for an example, suffering the vengeance of eternal fire" (Jude 7). The verb translated "giving themselves over to fornication"[10] is an intensified form of the standard word for committing sexual immorality. Sodom was guilty not merely of injustice and violence, but sexual sin. Similarly, 2 Peter 2:8 speaks of "the filthy conversation of the wicked" in

---

Peter H. Davids, *The Letters of 2 Peter and Jude*, Pillar New Testament Commentary (Grand Rapids: Eerdmans, 2006), 53.

8. Vines, *God and the Gay Christian*, 68.

9. White and Niell, *Same Sex Controversy*, 45–46.

10. Greek ἐκπορνεύω.

Sodom, where "filthy" refers to sexual licentiousness or shameless sensuality.[11]

Jude's phrase "strange flesh," literally, "other flesh,"[12] explains the nature of this sexual sin. Some commentators take this as a reference to lusting after angels. However, the men of Sodom did not know that the visitors were angels, nor does the Genesis account highlight lusting after angels as their crime, but their desire for sexual relations with "men" (Gen. 19:5).[13] Furthermore, Jude attributed this sin not to Sodom alone, but to the other nearby cities, though they were not visited by the angels.[14] Therefore, we should understand "strange flesh" as condemning them specifically for their homosexuality because of its violation of the boundaries of God's created order of sexuality.[15]

After Genesis, the Bible repeatedly refers to Sodom as an example of God's severe judgment on sinners.[16] Sodom stands as an eternal warning of

---

11. Greek ἀσέλγεια. See Rom. 13:13; Gal. 5:19; Eph. 4:19.

12. Greek σαρκὸς ἑτέρας.

13. The Hebrew term translated "men" in Gen. 19:5 is a generic word for man, sometimes used in a gender-specific manner (Gen. 6:4; 17:27; 19:4; 24:13).

14. DeYoung, *What Does the Bible Really Teach about Homosexuality?*, 38.

15. Davids, *The Letters of 2 Peter and Jude*, 52–53.

16. Deut. 29:23; Isa. 1:9–10; 3:9; 13:19; Jer. 23:14; 49:18; 50:40; Lam. 4:6; Ezek. 16:46–56; Amos 4:11; Zeph. 2:9; Matt. 10:15;

God's judgment on the sins of social injustice and homosexuality. The story of Sodom's attack on Lot and his guests does not merely function as an example of oppression and violation of the customs of hospitality, but as a notorious case of sexual lust—particularly homosexual lust.

The warning of the horrid example of Sodom is all the more explicit in God's holy law revealed through Moses and affirmed by Christ's apostles.

Homosexuality under the Law of God

The law of Moses clearly prohibited sexual acts between men. There are several references to male cult prostitutes serving in places of idolatry, which was strictly prohibited under the law of Moses.[17] The law also forbade all male-to-male sexual activity in general. Leviticus 18:22 says, "Thou shalt not lie with

---

11:23–24; Mark 6:11; Luke 10:12; 17:29; Rom. 9:29; 2 Peter 2:6; Jude 7; Rev. 11:8.

17. Deut. 23:17; 1 Kings 14:24; 15:12; 22:46; 2 Kings 23:7; Job 36:14. The term "sodomite" (קָדֵשׁ) literally means a male sacred person, or one set apart for religious purposes, but is generally translated "sodomite" in the KJV. Male prostitution to men was evidently a significant part of Canaanite religion. The feminine form (קְדֵשָׁה) is used for female cult prostitutes (Gen. 38:21–22; Deut. 23:17; Hos. 4:14). There is also the term "dog" (כֶּלֶב), used of a male temple prostitute (Deut. 23:18; cf. Rev. 22:15). See Gagnon, *The Bible and Homosexual Practice*, 100–110.

mankind, as with womankind: it is abomination."
Leviticus 20:13 says, "If a man also lie with mankind,
as he lieth with a woman, both of them have committed an abomination: they shall surely be put to
death; their blood shall be upon them."

Leviticus teaches that male homosexuality is
against God's law and the order of creation. The word
translated "mankind"[18] is the gender-specific term
translated *male* in Genesis 1:27 when God created
man in two genders: "male and female." To "lie with"
is another euphemism for sexual activity.[19] These laws
do not make any reference to prostitution, the age
of those involved, or any other circumstances; they
simply and directly forbid males having sexual relations with other males. They do not target one man
as an aggressor, but state of the homosexual partners
that "both of them have committed an abomination"
(Lev. 20:13).[20]

The phrase "as with a woman" points back to
the creation of the woman as a man's proper sexual
partner (Gen. 2:22–25). It in no way denigrates the
woman, whom the man needs as a helper sharing
his own nature (Gen. 2:18–20). The issue here is not
a patriarchal culture where a man may not lower

---

18. Hebrew זָכָר.

19. Hebrew שׁכב. See Gen. 19:32–35; 26:10; 30:15–16; 34:2, 7;
35:22; 39:7, 10, 12, 14; Ex. 22:16, 19; Lev. 15:18, 33, etc.

20. Hamilton, "How to Condone What the Bible Condemns," 37.

himself to the position of a woman, for Moses did not view women as inferior to men but as fellow sharers in the image of God (Gen. 1:27).[21] Instead, as Kevin DeYoung writes, "The reason the prohibitions are stated so absolutely, is because men were designed to have sex with women, not a man with another male."[22] Sexual relations between man and man, like sexual relations between man and animal, violate God's created order, frustrate His purposes for marriage and sexuality, and corrupt the image of God in man.[23]

God's law declares homosexual activity to be an "abomination." This word refers to something loathed or hated by God.[24] John Hartley comments, "Adultery,

---

21. Hamilton, "How to Condone What the Bible Condemns," 36. Contra Vines, *God and the Gay Christian*, 87–92; see also 108–110.

22. DeYoung, *What Does the Bible Really Teach about Homosexuality?*, 41.

23. "It should now be clear why incest, homosexuality, and bestiality are placed together in Leviticus 18. The rationale for proscribing all three is found not only in the pollution [unclean] rules, but also in their disregard of the purpose of creation. Unnatural acts, that is, cross-species and same-gender sexual relations, ultimately deny the creative work of God and offend the design of the human species, which is patterned after the image of God. Furthermore, these acts cannot fulfill the obligation to be fruitful and multiply." Wold, *Out of Order*, 131–32.

24. G. J. Wenham, *The Book of Leviticus*, New International Commentary on the Old Testament (Grand Rapids: Eerdmans, 1979), 259. In other contexts, this term (תּוֹעֵבָה) and its verbal root (תעב) can be used of a variety of objects, including idols

homosexuality, and bestiality are forbidden. Such sexual unions are confusing and repulsive. They destroy rather than enhance human dignity before God."[25] In this context, homosexuality is declared to be one of the activities for which God cast the Canaanites out of the land (Lev. 18:26–30). Homosexuality provokes the wrath of God against all nations. In the typology of the Old Testament, this points to the exclusion of those who engage in same-sex sexual activity from the kingdom of God.

Some object that Leviticus is full of all kinds of laws that Christians do not have to follow. For example, it also prohibits sexual relations with a woman unclean through her menstrual flow (Lev. 18:19). We are free from its regulations about foods and ceremonial cleanness. Why should we be bound by its regulations about homosexuality?[26]

We may answer this objection as follows.

---

and the worship of other gods (Deut. 7:25–26; 13:14; 17:4; 27:15; 32:16), child sacrifice (Deut. 12:31), unclean animals (Deut. 14:3), blemished sacrifices (Deut. 17:1), witchcraft (Deut. 18:9–12), and cheating on weights and measures (Deut. 25:13–16). This is not the same word as "abomination" (שֶׁקֶץ) with respect to Levitical laws of unclean animals (Lev. 11:10–13, 20, 23, 41–42). The latter is from a root meaning to be filthy.

25. John E. Hartley, *Leviticus*, Word Biblical Commentary 4 (Nashville: Thomas Nelson, 1992), 299.

26. Myers and Scanzoni, *What God Has Joined Together*, 89–90; Vines, *God and the Gay Christian*, 81–85.

1. Jesus taught us not to assume in general that the laws of God do not apply, but that they do apply (Matt. 5:17–19). The apostle Paul said that all Scripture, including all the Old Testament, is inspired of God for the spiritual profit of the Christian (2 Tim. 3:16).

2. The New Testament does not treat Leviticus as irrelevant, but quotes it repeatedly to give direction to the Christian life. The second greatest commandment, to love your neighbor as yourself, appears there (Lev. 19:18). In Leviticus, new covenant believers hear their call to be holy for the Lord is holy (Lev. 11:44–45; 1 Peter 1:16). The promise to Christians that if we repent of evil and walk in holiness, then God will dwell with us and be our God, is found in Leviticus (Lev. 26:11–12; 2 Cor. 6:16).

3. The law against sexual contact with a menstruating woman explicitly states that it relates not to moral evil but to "uncleanness" (Lev. 18:19), a category of the ceremonial law. The discharge of blood, though innocent in itself, fell under the restrictions of Israel's ceremonial cleanness required to live in God's presence (Lev. 15:19–31). The death of Christ released us from the ceremonial laws, and now they teach Christians to avoid *spiritual* uncleanness (2 Cor. 6:17). However, the law against males having sexual contact with males does not make any reference to ritual

cleanness, but makes a straightforward condemnation of a sexual sin alongside adultery and incest.[27]

4. Leviticus indicates that God judged the Canaanite peoples for sexual sins such as the abomination
of male-with-male intercourse, and cast them out
of the land (Lev. 18:22, 24–28; 20:13, 23). Therefore,
this prohibition was not limited to Israel. It did not
function merely as part of a ceremonial system that
distinguished Israel from other nations. Instead, it is
a moral obligation for which God holds all nations
accountable.[28]

5. The New Testament reaffirmed this old covenant
law, proving that it has abiding moral significance
for all peoples.[29] Christ and His apostles taught that
the law of God revealed to Moses continues to function to reveal sin and convict sinners of all kinds,

27. On these three points, see DeYoung, *What Does the Bible Really Teach about Homosexuality?*, 42–46.

28. White and Niell, *Same Sex Controversy*, 64–69.

29. The restatement of a law under the new covenant is not necessary to prove that it reveals God's abiding moral will, for the NT does not repeat the law against sexual contact with animals (Lev. 18:23; 20:15; Deut. 27:21), or the law against child sacrifice (Lev. 18:21), but both are God's will for mankind in all times and places. However, when such a law is restated, that confirms its binding nature across the ages.

including those practicing homosexuality. Paul wrote in 1 Timothy 1:9–10,

> Knowing this, that the law is not made for a righteous man, but for the lawless and disobedient, for the ungodly and for sinners, for unholy and profane, for murderers of fathers and murderers of mothers, for manslayers, for whoremongers, for them that defile themselves with mankind, for menstealers, for liars, for perjured persons, and if there be any other thing that is contrary to sound doctrine.

The phrase "them that defile themselves with mankind" translates a single masculine word[30] that combines two Greek terms, "male" and "bed," meaning, "males who go to bed [sexually] with males."[31] The same two terms appear in the ancient Greek

---

30. Greek ἀρσενοκοίτης, only here and 1 Cor. 6:9 in the NT and never in the LXX. Mounce writes that the word "is rare and does not appear to have existed before the time of Paul." William D. Mounce, *Pastoral Epistles*, Word Biblical Commentary 46 (Nashville: Thomas Nelson, 2000), 39.

31. Similar Greek words are formed with the -κοίτης ending, including "one who sleeps with slaves," "one who sleeps with his mother," and "one who sleeps with many." David F. Wright, "Homosexuals or Prostitutes? The Meaning of ΑΡΣΕΝΟΚΟΙΤΑΙ (1 Cor. 6:9, 1 Tim. 1:10)," *Vigiliae Christianae* 38, no. 2 (June 1984): 130. Vines's argument that the word refers to economic exploitation is remarkably weak. Vines, *God and the Gay Christian*, 122–25.

translation of both Leviticus 18:22 and 20:13, the laws against man-with-man sexual activity quoted above.[32] Therefore, Paul affirmed the abiding moral authority of the law's condemnation of homosexual acts. We cannot merely dismiss it as an old covenant ceremony; it is God's eternal, moral law.

Paul arranged this list of sins to reflect the order of the Ten Commandments:[33]

> 5. Honour thy father and thy mother.
> *murderers of fathers, murderers of mothers*

> 6. Thou shalt not kill.
> *manslayers*

> 7. Thou shalt not commit adultery.
> *whoremongers, them that defile themselves with men*

---

32. "καὶ μετὰ ἄρσενος οὐ κοιμηθήσῃ κοίτην γυναικός βδέλυγμα γάρ ἐστιν" (Lev. 18:22, LXX). "καὶ ὃς ἂν κοιμηθῇ μετὰ ἄρσενος κοίτην γυναικός βδέλυγμα ἐποίησαν ἀμφότεροι θανατούσθωσαν ἔνοχοί εἰσιν" (Lev. 20:3, LXX). Note that the two words ἄρσενος κοίτην appear side by side in the latter text, which Paul could easily have combined into ἀρσενοκοίτης. Wright comments, "The parallel between the LXX's ἄρσενος οὐ κοιμηθήσῃ κοίτην and even more κοιμηθῇ μετὰ ἄρσενος κοίτην and Paul's ἀρσενοκοῖται is surely inescapable." Wright, "Homosexuals or Prostitutes?", 129.

33. George W. Knight III, *Commentary on the Pastoral Epistles*, New International Greek Testament Commentary (Grand Rapids: Eerdmans, 1992), 83.

8. Thou shalt not steal.
   menstealers

9. Thou shalt not bear false witness.
   liars, perjured persons

By placing men who have sex with men immediately after "whoremongers" or fornicators in this list, he implied that the seventh commandment implicitly teaches that sexual relations must take place between a male husband and a female wife to whom the male is married, and not two persons of the same gender. Homosexuality violates the Ten Commandments.[34] In fact, just as murdering one's parents is an extreme form of not honoring them, and kidnapping (man-stealing) is an aggravated form of stealing, so homosexual acts may be listed here as an aggravated form of sexual immorality.

Therefore, the Old and New Testaments both affirm that the moral law of God forbids sexual activity between males. Such activity is an abomination to God, a violation of the principle of the seventh commandment, and a provocation of God's wrath and judgment.

---

34. Mounce, *Pastoral Epistles*, 38.

Jonathan and David: The Beauty of Non-Sexual Friendship

There has been a tendency among pro-homosexual writers to read any close relationship between persons of the same gender as a sexual relationship. The assumption seems to be that two men or two women cannot be good friends without getting into bed together. In reality, however, the Bible testifies to the goodness of a friend who is "closer than a brother" (Prov. 18:24).[35] For example, the apostle Paul had excellent friendships with a number of men and women without any sexual overtones.

The classic example of a beautiful, non-sexual friendship in the Bible is that of David and Jonathan.[36] Sadly, this too has been claimed as a homosexual partnership.[37] However, there is nothing sexual or erotic in scriptural accounts of their friendship. The Bible says, "The soul of Jonathan was knit with the soul of David" (1 Sam. 18:1a). The same language is used

---

35. See Joel R. Beeke and Michael A. G. Haykin, *How Should We Develop Biblical Friendship?*, Cultivating Biblical Godliness (Grand Rapids: Reformation Heritage Books, 2015).

36. For a careful analysis of the Hebrew Scriptures regarding this relationship, see Markus Zehnder, "Observations on the Relationship between David and Jonathan and the Debate on Homosexuality," *Westminster Theological Journal* 69, no. 1 (Spring 2007): 127–74. Portions of the article deal with matters some might find offensive.

37. Horner, *Jonathan Loved David*, 26–39.

of Jacob's love for his youngest son Benjamin (Gen. 44:30).[38] Scripture also says, "Jonathan loved him as his own soul" (1 Sam. 18:1b; cf. 20:17). This echoes God's love commandment, "Thou shalt love thy neighbor as thyself" (Lev. 19:18).[39] They made covenants of loyalty with each other (1 Sam. 18:3; 20:8, 16–17; 23:18). The demonstrations of their covenant love revolved around political loyalty because Jonathan recognized that God had appointed David to be the next king.[40] Jonathan gave David his weapons and robe as signs of his royal status. Jonathan protected David against the murderous envy of Jonathan's father King Saul. David showed royal favor to Jonathan's son Mephibosheth (1 Sam. 19–20; 23:16–18; 2 Sam. 9). They were also godly friends who delighted in each other's faith, humility, and company.

Two statements in particular about David and Jonathan have been twisted into declarations of homosexuality. First, when they said farewell because David must flee for his life, they kissed each other (1 Sam. 20:41). Men rarely kiss each other in North America, and so this strikes us as sexual. However, men commonly kissed as an expression of courtesy or affection in the Ancient Near East, as they do in

---

38. Zehnder, "Relationship between David and Jonathan," 140.
39. Zehnder, "Relationship between David and Jonathan," 146.
40. Gagnon, *The Bible and Homosexual Practice*, 147–51.

many cultures today. Jacob kissed his father Isaac and Laban kissed his nephew Jacob. Brothers kissed each other when adult men, at times with tears. Moses kissed his father-in-law. Samuel kissed Saul when he anointed him as king.[41] New Testament believers often greeted each other with a kiss.[42] Unless we would read all these as sexual relationships, we have no basis to see David and Jonathan, who were brothers-in-law, as expressing anything more than brotherly affection.

This point illustrates the importance of avoiding the modern "sexual orientation" category which we discussed earlier. In that erroneous theory, one's orientation is defined not only by one's erotic desires, but also by one's emotional bonds and social connections. When people operate under that assumption, a deep affection for a person of the same sex is assumed to indicate a homosexual orientation. This is another way in which modern culture attempts to make our sexual desires the master category that defines us. To avoid this confusion, we must recognize that friends of the same sex may have great affection and strong emotional bonds with each other without any sexual intent. Indeed, this is part of the image of God, who

---

41. Gen. 27:26–27; 29:13; 33:4; 45:15; Ex. 4:27; 18:7; 1 Sam. 10:1.
42. Rom. 16:16; 1 Cor. 16:20; 2 Cor. 13:12; 1 Thess. 5:26; 1 Peter 5:14.

affirmed His own relationality when He said, "Let *us* make man in *our* image" (Gen. 1:26).

Second, people claim that we see a homosexual relationship between Jonathan and David in David's lament when Saul and Jonathan fell in battle. After David lamented their deaths because they were mighty warriors for Israel, he said, "I am distressed for thee, my brother Jonathan: very pleasant hast thou been unto me: thy love to me was wonderful, passing the love of women" (2 Sam. 1:26). Some claim this to be a statement of David's sexuality. Here again, the comparison implies no sexual overtones,[43] only a poetic and perhaps hyperbolic statement that Jonathan had loved David more faithfully and sacrificially than his wives or possibly even his mother. Jonathan was heir to the king, but handed that right over to David.

Jonathan's love for David presents a marvelous model of a people's loyalty to their God-anointed king (1 Sam. 18:16). Rather than an example of homosexuality, this relationship is a type of the church's spiritual loyalty to the King of kings, Jesus Christ.

---

43. In Hos. 3:1, the Lord compares Hosea's love for his wife with the Lord's love for Israel, and yet the sexuality of the former does not imply any sexuality in the latter. Zehnder, "Relationship between David and Jonathan," 142.

Chapter 3

Expectations: The Power of Sin and the Power of Christ

Even if the Old Testament speaks against homosexuality, what about the New Testament? Doesn't the New Testament focus even more on the heart? How does the gospel of God's grace to sinners affect Christianity's approach to homosexuality?

A Diagnosis of Sexual Distortion

The longest and most detailed statement in the Bible about homosexuality is found in Paul's diagnosis in Romans 1 of the world's desperate need for the good news of God's power and righteousness for sinners in Jesus Christ. After stating that God is revealing His wrath or anger against all ungodliness and unrighteousness of men, Paul proceeded to explain how mankind knows of God's glory and goodness from His creations, but refuses to glorify and thank Him, and instead worships created things (Rom. 1:18–23).

The moral consequences unfolded in the remainder of chapter 1 are horrific. As one writer says, "Idolatry corrupts holy identity, which in turn leads to moral collapse."[1] God responded in wrath by giving idol-worshipers over to the power of their sins in three ways. The first is His handing them over to the power of sexual lust and uncleanness (Rom. 1:24–25).[2]

Paul described the second giving over as follows: "For this cause God gave them up unto vile affections: for even their women did change the natural use into that which is against nature: and likewise also the men, leaving the natural use of the woman, burned in their lust one toward another; men with men working that which is unseemly, and receiving in themselves that recompence of their error which was meet" (Rom. 1:26–27). Given the mention of the two genders, and the immediately preceding statements about sexual sin (v. 24), it is clear that Paul wrote of "natural

---

1. Anthony C. Thiselton, *The First Epistle to the Corinthians*, The New International Greek Testament Commentary (Grand Rapids: Eerdmans, 2000), 446. He cites Deut. 27–30; Hosea; Rom. 1:26–31; 1 Cor. 6:9–11.

2. Some commentators view the first and second as essentially the same, just further described and defined. Thus, John Murray, *The Epistle to the Romans*, The New International Commentary on the New Testament (Grand Rapids: Eerdmans, 1965), 46; Thomas R. Schreiner, *Romans*, Baker Exegetical Commentary on the New Testament (Grand Rapids: Baker Academic, 1998), 91.

use" with regard to sexual matters here.[3] There is not a hint in this text that Paul was speaking about abuse, or relationships between men and boys; like the laws of Leviticus, "homosexual relations in general are indicted," as Tom Schreiner observes.[4]

The third is His giving them over to a worthless mindset to commit all kinds of wickedness with approval even though they know God threatens such sins with death (Rom. 1:28–32).

The apostle makes the following points about homosexuality:

1. Sexual activity between persons of the same sex is *unnatural*. It is "against nature," a rebellion against the "natural use" of each gender. Sometimes it is claimed that "nature" refers to each individual's innate, personal nature, and so Paul was condemning people who act contrary to their sexual orientation.[5] However, "nature" refers here not to a personal orientation or inclination, but to God's created order for all mankind. The context in Romans 1 strongly emphasizes God as Creator and alludes to the early chapters of Genesis:

3. Schreiner also notes, "The word χρῆσις [use] is often used of sexual relations in Greek writings." Schreiner, *Romans*, 94.

4. Schreiner, *Romans*, 95–96.

5. Dan O. Via, cited in RPCNA, *Gospel and Sexual Orientation*, 51.

- "the creation of the world... the Creator" (Rom. 1:20, 25; cf. Gen. 1:1)

- "an image made like to... man... birds... beasts... creeping things" (Rom. 1:23; cf. Gen. 1:26, 30)

- "men... women," literally, "males... females" (Rom. 1:27; cf. Gen. 1:27)

- "the judgment of God, that they which commit such things are worthy of death" (Rom. 1:32; cf. Gen. 2:17).[6]

Paul used very gender-specific language here, "males" and "females," an allusion to God's creation of man in two distinct genders (Gen. 1:27).[7] God created each gender in such a way as to serve a distinct sexual function, functions reflected in the form of the body.[8] John Murray wrote, "The offense of homosexuality is the abandonment of the divinely constituted order in reference to sex."[9] Homosexuality exchanges the order set by the Creator for a disorder of its own making, just as mankind exchanges the glory

---

6. Gagnon, *The Bible and Homosexual Practice*, 289–91.

7. Greek θῆλυς and ἄρρην or ἄρσεν; see Gen. 1:27, LXX; Matt. 19:4; Mark 10:6.

8. The word "nature" (φύσις) and its cognates can have a physical connotation, referring to the body of a man, animal, or plant (Rom. 2:27; 11:21, 24; Gal. 2:15; James 3:7)

9. Murray, *The Epistle to the Romans*, 47–48.

of the Creator to worship His creatures (vv. 23, 25). Unnatural worship results in unnatural desires, and homosexuality is unnatural, as ancient Jews recognized.[10] Robert Gagnon concludes, "For Paul, both idolatry and same-sex intercourse reject God's verdict that what was made and arranged was 'very good' (Gen. 1:31)."[11]

2. God condemns sexual activity not only between men but also *between women*. The law of Moses explicitly forbade male-to-male sexual activity, but Paul included female-to-female relationships, though he gave more critical attention to the males.[12] This

---

10. The *Testament of Naphtali* (3.3–4), a Jewish writing of the second century BC, made this same connection: "The Gentiles, because they wandered astray and forsook the Lord, have changed the order, and have devoted themselves to stones and sticks…. But you, my children, shall not be like that… do not become like Sodom, which departed from the order of nature." Josephus said that the marriage of a man and a woman is "according to nature," but homosexual relations are against nature (παρὰ φύσιν). Quoted in Schreiner, *Romans*, 92, 96.

11. Gagnon, *The Bible and Homosexual Practice*, 291.

12. It may be significant that, while Paul did condemn both male and female homosexuality as unnatural and vile, he reserved his strongest critique for male homosexuality, perhaps indicating that male homosexuality has a greater tendency than lesbianism towards shameless behavior and sad consequences in this life. The promiscuity of male homosexuals is notorious. Statistical studies suggest that three-quarters or more of men who practice homosexuality have sexual relations with fifty or more

proves that Paul was not speaking of a specific form of homosexuality, such as man-boy relationships, for he addressed both male and female homosexuality.

3. Sexual *desires* towards the same sex are sin. The word "affection" (or passion) is closely linked in the New Testament with sexual desire.[13] The unusual Greek word translated "lust" means longing or desire.[14] The problem with these sexual desires is not that they are too strong. Scripture commends sexual desire in marriage so passionate as to be comparable to intoxication (Prov. 5:19).[15] The homosexual desires themselves are corrupt, being "vile" and "against nature" because it aims at what God forbids. Denny Burk explains, "The morally significant difference between sinful lust and benign desire is neither the intensity of the desire nor our own personal sense of

---

partners in their lifetimes, and a significant number with five hundred or more. Gagnon, *The Bible and Homosexual Practice*, 453–58. However, the "even" (τε) in "even their women" may express a sense of shock that the feminine gender would participate in such sin. Murray, *Epistle to the Romans*, 47.

13. Greek πάθος; see Col. 3:5; 1 Thess. 4:5.

14. Greek ὄρεξις, *hapax legomenon* in the NT, and thus not the same term as that used in Rom. 1:24 (ἐπιθυμία).

15. Contra Vines, who claims, "Paul wasn't condemning the expression of a same-sex orientation as opposed to the expression of an opposite sex orientation. He was condemning excess as opposed to moderation." Vines, *God and the Gay Christian*, 105.

its chosenness.... The difference is in the object of the desire."[16] Therefore, the Bible teaches that what today are called gay and lesbian desires and acts are sinful, whether the desires are temporary lust or a more stable "orientation," and whether the acts are unusual events or a long-term lifestyle.

This focus on desires gives a further clarification of the laws found in Leviticus. The law of Moses focused largely on actions, but also highlighted the heart, and Christ taught that the laws forbidding actions implied moral standards for the heart (Matt. 5:21–30). Likewise, Paul took the ancient laws forbidding same-sex sexual actions and applied them to the desires of the heart. If it is evil to do the act, then it is evil to desire it. Therefore, repentance requires not only changing our behavior, but fighting to put evil desires to death (Col. 3:5). We must recognize that the fall of man has brought corruption to the deepest desires of our hearts (Gen. 6:5; Mark 7:20–23), and the restoration of man to God's image must transform our inner being (Eph. 4:22–24). This process of sanctification is neither quick nor easy, but only possible by continually looking to Christ as the One who died and rose again to be our life (Col. 3:1–4).

---

16. Burk, "Is Homosexual Orientation Sin," 101.

4. The Scriptures define gender and righteous sexuality *not in terms of a personal perception of sexual orientation, but as God's created order*. Paul's words apply to any sexual desire or action towards the same gender, regardless of whether the person feels his sexuality to be inclined towards the other gender, the same gender, or whatever. The question that the Bible addresses is not, "What is your orientation?" but, "Have you desired or done anything contrary to God's created order for sexuality?" The apostle is teaching us that we should not define our identity upon our desires or a felt orientation, but upon the natural order of creation, including the genders established by the Creator. That order, revealed in Genesis, requires us to direct our sexual desires and actions toward the other gender, a man to his wife and a woman to her husband.

5. Homosexual desires and actions *degrade human beings*. They are "vile," which means they bring dishonor to those who exercise them.[17] They produce "that which is unseemly," that is, indecency and cause for shame.[18] Earlier Paul had said of sexual sin that it dishonors the bodies of those who do it (v. 24; cf. 1 Cor. 6:18). Homosexuality aggravates and intensifies

---

17. Greek ἀτιμία.
18. Greek ἀσχημοσύνη; see Rev. 16:15.

this dishonor because it is unnatural, and thus distorts human nature as God created it to be. Refusing to glorify God leads to disgraceful desires and conduct.[19] Paul went on to say that such people are already receiving the penalty which necessarily accompanies such a wandering from God's ways.[20] Homosexual activity is not a pathway to liberty, but to degradation. In a fallen world, we must judge what is good for people based upon God's Word, not human feelings.

6. Homosexuality particularly manifests itself in an *idolatrous people* who have turned from the knowledge of the true God. It is significant that the text uses plurals to refer to a group. Paul does not say that each individual who engages in such sins is particularly idolatrous, but rather that when a people or nation turns from the Creator to worship idols, God gives that people over to greater bondage to fornication and homosexuality. He was "not talking about an individual's decline into sin," but giving "a typical

---

19. Schreiner, *Romans*, 92. Note the contrast between "vile" (dishonor) and "glorify/glory" (vv. 21, 23).

20. The verb translated "receiving" is a Greek present participle, suggesting a continuing action. "Was meet" translates a verb literally meaning "it is necessary" (δεῖ). It may be that the "error" or wandering consists of idolatry, and the punishment is homosexual activity itself in its degenerate desires, dishonor, and degradation. Thus Murray, *Epistle to the Romans*, 48.

description of a culture's decline."[21] This explains why homosexuality was largely a trait of the pagan Gentile world, and not of Israel except insofar as they degenerated away from the true worship of the Lord.[22] Homosexuality not only provokes the wrath of God, but it is a sign that the wrath of God has already come upon an idolatrous people.

In summary, Paul's epistle to the Romans declares both male-to-male and female-to-female sexuality as unnatural and degrading, a violation of God's created order that springs from a society warped by rebellion against our Creator.

Homosexuality and Salvation in Christ

Paul did not write Romans 1 in order to proudly judge homosexuality, or to cast those practicing it or struggling against it into despair, but as part of a larger diagnosis of mankind's need for the gospel of Jesus Christ (Rom. 1:16–17; 3:21–26). The most shocking news of the epistle to the Romans is that God loves sinners, both immoral pagans (Rom. 1:18–32)

---

21. RPCNA, *Gospel and Sexual Orientation*, 18.

22. Thus, the repeat of the sin of Sodom by the Israelite men of Gibeah (Judg. 19:22) represented the apostasy of Israel from the Lord and epitomized a society that rejected God's law, and lived in lawless autonomy so that "every man did that which was right in his own eyes" (Judg. 17:6; 21:25).

and self-righteous religious hypocrites (Rom. 2), and sent Christ to die for His enemies in order to rescue and reconcile them.

Paul's message of law and gospel for people who have given themselves over to same-sex erotic desires and practices comes through most clearly in 1 Corinthians 6:9–11, where he wrote, "Know ye not that the unrighteous shall not inherit the kingdom of God? Be not deceived: neither fornicators, nor idolaters, nor adulterers, nor effeminate, nor abusers of themselves with mankind, nor thieves, nor covetous, nor drunkards, nor revilers, nor extortioners, shall inherit the kingdom of God. And such were some of you: but ye are washed, but ye are sanctified, but ye are justified in the name of the Lord Jesus, and by the Spirit of our God."

Paul reiterated the law of God that homosexuality is sin. The phrase "abusers of themselves with mankind" translates the same Greek word seen before in 1 Timothy 1:10, which means "men who go to bed with males."[23] Here again the word echoes the laws of Leviticus in its condemnation of all sexual activity between men, a connection strengthened by the fact that Paul had just written strongly against incest, another sexual sin condemned in Leviticus

---

23. Greek ἀρσενοκοίτης.

18 and 20.[24] The word translated "effeminate" literally means "soft," here "men who are soft."[25] Immediately preceding "men who go to bed with males," it refers to men who seek to attract and please homosexual aggressors.[26]

These two words encompass the full range of male homosexual behavior, and rebuke it as sin incompatible with Christianity. We cannot assume that Paul only condemned the abuse of teenage boys or slaves because he was ignorant of homosexual relationships involving more equality or affection; the apostle's life and ministry in cities steeped in Greco-Roman culture would have acquainted him with the wide variety of male-to-male sexual relationships practiced in the ancient world.[27] He did not specify man-boy relationships; his language is broad enough to include all kinds of male homosexual activity as

---

24. David E. Garland, *1 Corinthians*, Baker Exegetical Commentary on the New Testament (Grand Rapids: Baker Academic, 2003), 212–13.

25. Greek μαλακός; see Matt. 11:8; Luke 7:25.

26. Gordon D. Fee, *The First Epistle to the Corinthians*, The New International Commentary on the New Testament (Grand Rapids: Eerdmans, 1987), 243–44.

27. "Paul witnessed around him both abusive relationships of power or money and examples of 'genuine love' between males.... Wolff carefully shows that Paul's situation in cosmopolitan pluralistic cultures made him aware of what are not simply 'modern' shades of distinction." Thiselton, *First Epistle to the Corinthians*, 452.

unrighteous. Mohler writes, "Biblical Christianity can neither endorse same-sex marriage nor accept the claim that a believer can be obedient to Christ and remain or persist in same-sex behaviors."[28]

Such men who do not repent of their sin will not "inherit the kingdom of God." In the teaching of Jesus Christ, the only alternative to inheriting the kingdom is being cast into the fires of hell for eternal punishment.[29] We dare not focus this warning entirely upon people who practice homosexual sins and ignore the many sins which, if habitual displays of the heart's character, will damn sinners to hell. On the other hand, we cannot fail to warn people who participate in same-sex erotic activity that they must repent of such desires and acts if they would live forever in God's kingdom. To pronounce God's blessing on the union of two men or two women is to endanger their souls. DeYoung says, "Solemnizing same-sex sexual behavior—like supporting any form of sexual immorality—runs the risk of leading people to hell."[30]

However, here we also see the gospel of God's power and righteousness in Jesus Christ. Paul did not write that if we ever commit such sins then we

---

28. Mohler, "God, the Gospel and the Gay Challenge," 22.

29. Matt. 25:34, 41, 46; cf. Rev. 21:7–8.

30. DeYoung, *What Does the Bible Really Teach about Homosexuality?*, 77.

are surely damned, but he said, "And such were some of you." Some Corinthian believers had lived as such sinners, but the past tense indicates that they are no longer unrighteous—no longer adulterers, men who sleep with men, thieves, or drunkards.[31] Their fundamental identity has changed because they are "in Christ Jesus" (1 Cor. 1:2). Union with Christ now defines them, and they cannot be the same.[32]

This change did not arise from themselves, but by the work of God through Christ by the Holy Spirit. Paul described it in three words: washed, sanctified, and justified.[33]

- Spiritual *washing*, pictured outwardly in the waters of baptism (Acts 22:16), is the Spirit's cleansing of the filth that dominated the sinner's soul, a personal application of the death of Christ in regeneration (Eph. 5:25–26; Titus 3:3–6; Rev. 1:5).

---

31. The Greek tense is imperfect, implying a condition that continued in the past, or actions repeated in the past.

32. "Their identities had been forever changed in Jesus Christ such that they were not now to be known by those same-sex identities any more than the sober man or the former thief would be known as a drunkard or thief." RPCNA, *Gospel and Sexual Orientation*, 47.

33. It is possible that the three words reflect the promises of Ezekiel 36: cleansing with clean water from filth and idols (v. 25), a new heart and the indwelling Spirit (vv. 26–27), and the blessing of the covenant relationship (v. 28).

- *Sanctification* in this case refers not to the process of Christian growth but a definite work at conversion. It is the work of the Spirit to set apart the person as holy unto God, so that he is now a saint of God (1 Cor. 1:2; 2 Cor. 1:1).

- *Justification* is not a change in the person's soul, but in his legal status, so that God counts him as righteous by faith alone because Christ died for his sins and rose again as his living righteousness (Rom. 3:21–26; 4:25; Gal. 2:16; Phil. 3:9).

The good news for those convinced of the sinfulness of homosexual desires and practice is that Christ does change people for His glory. Telling people that Christ can save them from sin is not homophobia. True homophobia is believing that people who practice same-sex sexual relations are so different that they can never turn back to the Lord and His ways.[34] Therefore, the homosexual man or woman who repents and trusts in Christ by grace may say, "I once was a person ruled by same-sex desires, but that is not my identity any longer. I am not dirty and defiled, but washed and clean. I am not unholy and profane, but sanctified as a saint of God. I am not

---

34. Butterfield, *Secret Thoughts of an Unlikely Convert*, 169.

guilty and condemned, but justified and vindicated by the perfect obedience of Christ."

That is not to say that he feels no more homosexual temptations and never sins again, or that he does not need the help of brothers and sisters in Christ and a diligent use of the means of grace to grow. Every Christian experiences an inward battle against remaining sin, a conflict between a heart that loves God's law and the evil still present in him (Rom. 7:14–23; Gal. 5:17; 1 Peter 2:11). At times this battle makes him cry out to God in sorrow over the sinful desires waging war against his soul.

We recognize that some people may have a personal disposition that makes them more inclined towards homosexuality than other people, just as each person tends towards some sins more than other sins. Jonathan Edwards wrote regarding the new birth,

> Indeed allowances must be made for the natural temper: conversion doesn't entirely root out the natural temper: those sins which a man by his natural constitution was most inclined to before his conversion, he may be most apt to fall into still. But yet conversion will make a great alteration even with respect to these sins. Though grace, while imperfect, doesn't root out an evil natural temper; yet it is of great power and efficacy with respect to it, to correct

it.... If a man before his conversion, was by his natural constitution, especially inclined to lasciviousness, or drunkenness, or maliciousness; converting grace will make a great alteration in him, with respect to these evil dispositions; so that however he may be still most in danger of these sins, yet they shall no longer have dominion over him; nor will they any more be properly his character.[35]

The gospel promise of "such *were* some of you" means there is no such thing as a gay Christian or a lesbian Christian, any more than there is a Christian adulterer or a Christian drunkard. The Christian is a new creation, for the death and resurrection of Jesus Christ have decisively overcome the guilt and power of sin (Rom. 6:1–14; 2 Cor. 5:17; Eph. 2:1–10). The answer to the conflict is not to try to legitimize sinful desires, but to cling by faith to the promises of Christ and who you are in Him.

Our culture would define us by the direction of our desires (sexual orientation), but only God has the right to define us, and He does so by our created gender (biological sex) and redeemed status in Jesus Christ. This new identity in Christ becomes the basis

---

35. *The Works of Jonathan Edwards, Volume 2, Religious Affections*, ed. John E. Smith (New Haven: Yale University Press, 1959), 341–42. We are indebted for this reference to RPCNA, *The Gospel and Sexual Orientation*, 19.

for new obedience, and must be appropriated daily by trusting in the promises of the gospel. The battle then is to become what you are in Christ: washed, sanctified, and justified.[36]

The battle is fought in the context of a local church that accepts repentant sinners no matter what they once were, and surrounds them with prayer, brotherly love, accountability, and exhortation. Paul did not address this letter to an isolated individual, but to a community of believers, "the church of God which is at Corinth," whom God had called "unto the fellowship of his Son Jesus Christ our Lord," fellowship with Christ and fellowship in Christ with each other (1 Cor. 1:2, 9). He reminded them they are organically joined together by Christ's Spirit like members of the human body, and they need each other (1 Cor. 12:12–22).

Christians need to remember that the identity of those who practice same-sex erotic activity is often bound up in a community of like-minded persons because of the acceptance found there.[37] As one person said, "I'm a gay man because the GLBT (Gay,

---

36. Fee, *First Epistle to the Corinthians*, 247.

37. "Sexual orientation also refers to a person's sense of identity based on those attractions, related behaviors, and membership in a community of others who share those attractions." American Psychological Association, *Answers...Sexual Orientation and Homosexuality*, 1.

Lesbian, Bisexual and Transgendered) community is the only safe home I have."[38] The church must be willing to welcome friends and visitors who identify themselves as homosexual, bisexual, or transgender. We must show them warmth, respect, and love in order to demonstrate that biblical Christianity is not a club for self-righteous, judgmental hypocrites, but a fellowship of repentant sinners who are growing saints. Church must be safe, not safe for sin, but safe for people who sin.

For those saved from sin, building a new sense of identity in Christ entails building new relationships in the community of Christ. Through wholesome fellowship and godly companionship with people of both genders, new Christians grow in their experiential knowledge of Christ and His ways, meet many of their emotional and social needs, and serve others through the sacrificial use of their gifts.[39] If we will love and serve them with patience, we can have the joy of seeing them not only overcome homosexual sins, but grow holistically as persons created and renewed in God's image.

38. Quoted in Butterfield, *Secret Thoughts of an Unlikely Convert*, 50.

39. RPCNA, *Gospel and Sexual Orientation*, 63–64.

Chapter 4

Conclusions:
Grace and Truth

Many voices around us celebrate homosexual love and relationships. The rainbow, originally chosen by God as a sign of His grace and patience towards a sinful race (Gen. 9), has become a symbol of a movement demanding acceptance and condemning all who oppose homosexual activity as sin. Love, they tell us, requires unconditional acceptance of all forms of sexuality so long as it does not hurt anyone. However, God did not merely tell us to love people, but explained what love means in many commandments in the Bible. We cannot throw away God's Word in the name of love, but must learn what God commands, and obey Him in love.

The Bible grounds our understanding of ourselves in the account of our creation by God. God made man in His image, male and female in relationship as husband and wife. Our identity, sexuality, and gender find their definitions in God's created order and redemptive work in Jesus Christ. No man or woman, no matter how highly placed or highly regarded, has the authority to tell us who we are. Only God can do that, and He has defined marriage as the joining together of one man and one woman in mutual commitment and sexual oneness.

The Old Testament reveals God's displeasure against sexual sin, including homosexual sin. The destruction of the notorious city of Sodom by God's fiery wrath stands as an enduring testimony of God's anger against injustice and homosexuality. The laws of holiness explicitly forbade man having sex with men. Instead, the Old Testament holds up as models honorable men in close, brotherly friendships like Jonathan and David.

The New Testament reaffirmed the laws of the Old, showing how homosexuality rebels against God's created order even in its sexual desires for the same gender. It places both male and female homosexuality with other sins under the condemnation of God as a symptom of a society given to proud idolatry instead of grateful worship of the Creator. Nevertheless, the gospel offers Christ to those who practice homosexuality, the Christ who can wash them, sanctify them, and justify them. The good news that Christians proclaim is not heterosexuality, but Jesus Christ, the Savior of His people from all sins. The Lord Jesus came neither to declare that "love wins," nor to promote bigotry, but as God's Son "full of grace and truth" (John 1:14).

This study has richly confirmed the biblical basis of our Reformed confessional heritage. On the basis of the biblical truths discussed in this booklet, we can confidently affirm what the Westminster Confession of Faith says: "Marriage is to be between one man and one woman."[1] We may also boldly declare the warning of the Westminster Larger Catechism, when it says that "sodomy, and all unnatural lusts (Rom. 1:24, 26–27; Lev. 20:15–16)" are sins "forbidden in the seventh commandment."[2] Both homosexual activity and desire violate God's holy law.[3] As with other sins against God's law, people must repent of homosexuality and be converted, or they will "by no means...inherit the kingdom of God," as the Heidelberg Catechism states.[4]

---

1. Westminster Confession of Faith (24.1), in *Reformed Confessions*, 4:263. The same statement appears in the London Baptist Confession (25.1) as well (4:561).

2. Westminster Larger Catechism (Q. 139), in *Reformed Confessions*, 4:333.

3. RPCNA, *Gospel and Sexual Orientation*, 54.

4. "Cannot they then be saved, who, continuing in their wicked and ungrateful lives, are not converted to God? By no means; for the Holy Scripture declares that no unchaste person, idolater, adulterer, thief, covetous man, drunkard, slanderer, robber, or any such like, shall inherit the kingdom of God." Heidelberg Catechism, LD 32, Q. 87, in *Doctrinal Standards, Liturgy, and Church Order*, ed. Joel R. Beeke (Grand Rapids: Reformation Heritage Books,

We must lovingly proclaim the good news to all sinners, that God calls them to come to Christ, and all who have true faith in Jesus Christ are fully forgiven and "through the virtue of Christ's death and resurrection… the dominion of the whole body of sin is destroyed, and the several lusts thereof are more and more weakened and mortified…to the practice of true holiness," as the confession says.[5] Live by faith in the Son of God, and though you will have to fight daily against evil desires—we all do—you will also know His love and power.

In a world where some boldly assert their sexual identity and orientation contrary to Scripture, others wrestle with doubts and questions about who they are, and yet others quietly and faithfully fight

---

2003), 66. Though the Heidelberg Catechism does not explicitly name sodomy or homosexuality, it clearly includes it under "any such like," as the reference to 1 Cor. 6:9–10 implies. See Kevin DeYoung, "Does the Heidelberg Catechism Have Anything to Say about Homosexuality?" *The Gospel Coalition* blog, March 16, 2002, accessed August 18, 2015, http://www.thegospelcoalition.org/blogs/kevindeyoung/2012/03/16/does-the-heidelberg-catechism-have-anything-to-say-about-homosexuality/. The same was affirmed by early Particular Baptists in their adaptation of the Heidelberg Catechism. See Hercules Collins, *An Orthodox Catechism*, ed. Michael A. G. Haykin and G. Stephen Weaver, Jr. (Palmsdale, Cal.: RBAP, 2014), 92.

5. Westminster Confession of Faith (13.1), in *Reformed Confessions*, 4:249. The same statement appears in the London Baptist Confession (13.1) as well (4:548).

against desires they know to be sinful, we find liberty in believing the Word of God. Burk writes, "In God's world, we are who God says we are. We are not merely the sum total of our fallen sexual desires."[6] Do not let the world, the flesh, or the devil define you. If you are in Christ, then you are not a slave of anything on earth. Christian, your identity is that of a servant of God by creation, a sinner against God by the fall, a son of God by redemption, and a saint of God by His call. Paul puts it this way in Romans 6:11–12: "Reckon ye also yourselves to be dead indeed unto sin, but alive unto God through Jesus Christ our Lord. Let not sin therefore rein in your mortal body, that ye should obey it in the lusts thereof."

We also hope that the Bible's strong words would discourage no one from developing close same-sex friendships that are chaste and pure. There is nothing wrong with having close friendships with people of the same gender.[7] The modern idea of sexual orientation is confusing in this regard, for it defines one's orientation not just by sexual desires but emotional connections, psychological self-perception, and social networks. It suggests that there is something "gay" about being a dear friend of a person of the same sex. However, as seen in David and Jonathan

---

6. Burk, "Is Homosexual Orientation Sinful?", 113.
7. Butterfield, *Openness Unhindered*, 121.

and many other friendships, we can enjoy holy, God-honoring, affectionate, non-sexual relationships with persons of the same gender.[8] The church should cultivate such friendships in its midst.

The church must also welcome those identifying themselves as LGBT into our lives and worship services, love them, befriend them, listen to them, teach them, warn them, and serve them. In a polarized and politicized environment, both Christians and "gays" may be surprised to discover each other to be real human beings.[9] Love is not compromise, but the very heart of holiness. When those involved in homosexuality (and other sins) turn to Christ in true faith and repentance by the Spirit's grace, we must then welcome them into the membership of the church and not treat them as second-class Christians if they continue to struggle against their old sinful desires. Remember how much we do too.

Lastly, let us never forget that Christ's call to repentance is not limited to any class or category of sinners. Repentance is the essence of the Christian life from beginning to end. We call mankind to repent for the same reason that Christ did: love for sinners. Heath Lambert says, "Love requires a tender

---

8. Burk, "Is Homosexual Orientation Sinful?", 112.

9. See Glenn T. Stanton, *Loving My (LGBT) Neighbor: Being Friends in Grace and Truth* (Chicago: Moody, 2014)

call to repentance. A life devoid of repentance is a life devoid of Christ."[10] Whoever you may be, when the church calls you to repent, understand that it calls you to join us as we repent too.

Concluding Summary Statement on Homosexuality

God commands us to love our neighbor as ourselves (Lev. 19:18), and does not exclude any category of human beings from that love, including those who are evil and those who hate us (Matt. 5:44–48). Yet love is not our only rule, for God teaches us what love means through the many commandments of His Word (John 14:15; 1 John 5:2). The Holy Scriptures of the Old and New Testaments are inspired of God and sufficient to guide us in all matters of faith and obedience (2 Tim. 3:16–17). Gender, healthy sexuality, and marriage are not defined by humanity, but by the Creator to whom we must submit, as Christ said in His teaching about marriage (Matt. 19:4–6).

Being committed to the Bible as the Word of Christ, we and our churches must confess that the Holy Scriptures teach the following:

---

10. Lambert, "Is a 'Gay Christian' Consistent with the Gospel of Christ?" in *Response to Matthew Vines*, 79.

- God created mankind in His image, with two distinct and equally valuable genders, male and female, in accordance with their biological sex (Gen. 1:27). It is against God's will to identify one's gender in a manner contrary to biology (Deut. 22:5).

- God instituted marriage as the union of one man and one woman (Gen. 2:24), outside of which all other sexual activity is condemned by God (Ex. 20:14; Eph. 5:5–6).

- God condemns homosexuality as a sin that offends Him. This is evident in the destruction of Sodom (Gen. 19; Jude 7), the Old Testament law of holiness (Lev. 18:22; 20:13), and the New Testament affirmation of that law (1 Tim. 1:9–10).

- God's condemnation extends to all homosexual desires and acts, by males or females, for it is against God's created order (Rom. 1:26–27).

- Spontaneous attractions or perceived sexual orientation in any way contrary to God's Word are sinful, for the inclinations or first motions of original corruption in the soul are sin and evil, even apart from a conscious choice (Gen. 6:5; 8:21; Rom. 7:20–21).

- Unrepentant sinners, including fornicators, adulterers, and those who practice homosexuality, have no place in God's kingdom (1 Cor. 6:9–10). All who refuse to repent will face the righteous judgment of God on the day of His wrath (Rom. 2:5).

- In His sovereign, electing love, God loves sinners of all kinds, including those who practice homosexuality (Matt. 5:45; John 3:16). He forgives and changes those whom He saves so that they have a new identity in Christ as saints sanctified to God by His amazing grace (1 Cor. 1:2, 30; 6:11).

- True Christians experience an inner conflict between sinful and holy desires (Gal. 5:17), but sin no longer defines who they are, nor does it rule them (Rom. 6:11, 14). Their calling is to hope in Christ and fight against every evil desire (Col. 3:1, 5).

In making this statement, we do not endorse any injustice, violence, or self-righteousness toward people regardless of their identity or manner of life. We highly value all human beings, and are committed to treating them with honor and kindness even if they persist in sin (1 Peter 2:17; 3:9–11). We commit ourselves to welcoming all who are willing to hear the preaching of God's Word, to embracing as brothers and sisters in Christ all who repent and trust in

Jesus Christ alone for salvation, and to enfolding in our compassionate spiritual care all who join us in seeking grace and strength to flee from lust, pursue peace and holiness, and live as pilgrims on the way to Christ's kingdom.

Christ comes with grace and truth for sinners (Luke 5:32; John 1:14). Homosexual desires and acts are not the only sins, nor the worst sin, for it is not the unpardonable sin. Since it can be repented of by grace, it need not inevitably lead to damnation. We confess our own sinfulness and worthiness of hell. Christ died for sinners and rose again—and He is our only hope. Our call to men and women who rejoice in same-sex erotic desires or who participate in same-sex erotic activity is the same as our call to all sinners: repent of your sins and believe in the Lord Jesus Christ, and you shall be saved (Mark 1:15; Acts 16:31).

Bibliography of Works Cited

Allberry, Sam. *Is God Anti-gay? And Other Questions about Homosexuality, the Bible and Same-Sex Attraction.* Epsom, Surrey, U.K.: The Good Book Company, 2013.

American Psychiatric Association, "Position Statement on Issues Related to Homosexuality." 2013. Accessed August 5, 2015, http://www.psychiatry .org/File%20Library/Learn/Archives/Position-2013-Homosexuality.pdf.

American Psychological Association, *Answers to Your Questions: For a Better Understanding of Sexual Orientation and Homosexuality.* Washington, D.C.: American Psychological Association, 2008, accessed August 4, 2015, https://www.apa.org/topics /lgbt/orientation.pdf.

The Associated Press Stylebook and Briefing on Media Law, 2013. New York: Basic Books, 2013.

Beeke, Joel R. and Michael A. G. Haykin. *How Should We Develop Biblical Friendship*, Cultivating Biblical Godliness. Grand Rapids: Reformation Heritage Books, 2015.

Brown, Michael L. *Can You Be Gay and Christian? Responding with Love and Truth to Questions about Homosexuality*. Lake Mary, Fla.: Charisma House, 2014.

Burk, Denny. "Is Homosexual Orientation Sin?" *Journal of the Evangelical Theological Society* 58, no. 1 (2015): 95–115.

Butterfield, Rosaria Champagne. *Openness Unhindered: Further Thoughts of an Unlikely Convert on Sexual Identity and Union with Christ*. Pittsburgh: Crown and Covenant, 2015.

———. *The Secret Thoughts of an Unlikely Convert: An English Professor's Journey into Christian Faith*. Expanded Edition. Pittsburgh: Crown and Covenant, 2015.

Christopher, Mark. *Same-sex Marriage: Is It Really the Same?* Leominster, U.K.: Day One, 2009.

Collins, Hercules. *An Orthodox Catechism*, edited by Michael A. G. Haykin and G. Stephen Weaver, Jr. Palmsdale, Cal.: RBAP, 2014.

Davids, Peter H. *The Letters of 2 Peter and Jude*, Pillar New Testament Commentary. Grand Rapids: Eerdmans, 2006.

Dennison, James T., compiler. *Reformed Confessions of the Sixteenth and Seventeenth Centuries in English Translation: Volume 4, 1600–1693*. Grand Rapids: Reformation Heritage Books, 2014.

DeYoung, Kevin. "Does the Heidelberg Catechism Have Anything to Say about Homosexuality?" *The Gospel Coalition* blog, March 16, 2002, accessed August 18, 2015, http://www.thegospelcoalition

.org/blogs/kevindeyoung/2012/03/16/does-the
-heidelberg-catechism-have-anything-to-say
-about-homosexuality/.

———. *What Does the Bible Really Teach about Homosexuality?* Wheaton, Ill.: Crossway, 2015.

Diamond, Lisa M. "Just How Different are Female and Male Sexual Orientation?" video lecture, October 17, 2013, *Cornell University*, accessed August 7, 2015, http://www.cornell.edu/video/lisa-diamond-on-sexual-fluidity-of-men-and-women.

———. *Sexual Fluidity: Understanding Women's Love and Desire*. Cambridge: Mass.: Harvard University Press, 2009.

Doctrinal Standards, Liturgy, and Church Order, ed. Joel R. Beeke. Grand Rapids: Reformation Heritage Books, 2003.

Edwards, Jonathan. *The Works of Jonathan Edwards, Volume 2, Religious Affections*, edited by John E. Smith. New Haven: Yale University Press, 1959.

Fee, Gordon D. *The First Epistle to the Corinthians*, The New International Commentary on the New Testament. Grand Rapids: Eerdmans, 1987.

Gagnon, Robert A. J. *The Bible and Homosexual Practice: Texts and Hermeneutics*. Nashville: Abingdon Press, 2001.

Garland, David E. *1 Corinthians*, Baker Exegetical Commentary on the New Testament. Grand Rapids: Baker Academic, 2003.

Hamilton, Victor P. *The Book of Genesis, Chapters 18–50*, New International Commentary on the Old Testament. Grand Rapids: Eerdmans, 1995.

Hannon, Michael W. "Against Heterosexuality: The Idea of Sexual Orientation Is Artificial and Inhibits Christian Witness." *First Things*, no. 241 (March 2014): 27–34.

Hartley, John E. *Leviticus*, Word Biblical Commentary 4. Nashville: Thomas Nelson, 1992.

Horner, Tom. *Jonathan Loved David: Homosexuality in Biblical Times*. Philadelphia: Westminster Press, 1978.

Jones, Stanton L. and Mark A. Yarhouse. *Ex-Gays? A Longitudinal Study of Religiously Mediated Change in Sexual Orientation*. Downers Grove, Ill.: IVP Academic, 2007.

Knight, George W. III. *Commentary on the Pastoral Epistles*, New International Greek Testament Commentary. Grand Rapids: Eerdmans, 1992.

Kort, Joe. "Going with the Flow: Male and Female Sexual Fluidity." *Huffington Post: Gay Voices*, updated 4/10/2015, accessed August 7, 2015, http://www.huffingtonpost.com/joe-kort-phd/going-with-the-flow-male-_b_6642504.html.

Mohler, R. Albert Jr., *We Cannot Be Silent: Speaking Truth to a Culture Redefining Sex, Marriage, and the Very Meaning of Right and Wrong*. Nashville: Thomas Nelson, 2015.

Mohler, R. Albert Jr., editor. *God and the Gay Christian? A Response to Matthew Vines*. Louisville, Ky.: SBTS Press, 2014, ebook, accessed August 4, 2015, http://sbts.me/ebook.

Mollenkott, Virginia R. *Omnigender: A Trans-Religious Approach*. Cleveland: Pilgrim Press, 2001.

Mounce, William D. *Pastoral Epistles*, Word Biblical Commentary 46. Nashville: Thomas Nelson, 2000.

Murray, John. *The Epistle to the Romans*, The New International Commentary on the New Testament. Grand Rapids: Eerdmans, 1965.

Ortlund, Raymond C., Jr. "Male-Female Equality and Male Headship: Genesis 1-3." In *Recovering Biblical Manhood and Womanhood: A Response to Evangelical Feminism*, edited by John Piper and Wayne Grudem, 95-112. Wheaton, Ill.: Crossway Books, 1991.

Paton, Lewis B. "The Holiness-Code and Ezekiel." *Presbyterian and Reformed Review* 7, no. 25 (January 1896): 98-115.

Pearcey, Nancy R. *Total Truth: Liberating Christianity from Its Cultural Captivity*. Wheaton, Ill.: Crossway, 2004.

Petersen, William L. "Can ΑΡΣΕΝΟΚΟΙΤΑΙ Be Translated by 'Homosexuals'?" *Vigiliae Christianae* 40, no. 2 (June 1986): 187-91.

Pronk, Pim. *Against Nature? Types of Moral Argumentation Regarding Homosexuality*, translated by John Vriend. Grand Rapids: Eerdmans, 1993.

Scanzoni, Letha Dawson and Virginia Ramey Mollenkott, *Is the Homosexual My Neighbor? A Positive Christian Response*. Revised Edition. New York: HarperCollins, 1994.

Schreiner, Thomas R. *Romans*, Baker Exegetical Commentary on the New Testament. Grand Rapids: Baker Academic, 1998.

Stanton, Glenn T. *Loving My (LGBT) Neighbor: Being Friends in Grace and Truth*. Chicago: Moody, 2014.

Synod of the Reformed Presbyterian Church in North America. *The Gospel and Sexual Orientation*, edited by Michael Lefebvre. Pittsburgh: Crown and Covenant, 2012.

Thiselton, Anthony C. *The First Epistle to the Corinthians*, The New International Greek Testament Commentary. Grand Rapids: Eerdmans, 2000.

White, James R. and Jeffrey D. Niell, *The Same Sex Controversy*. Bloomington, Minn.: Bethany House, 2002.

Via, Dan. O. and Robert A. J. Gagnon, *Homosexuality and the Bible: Two Views*. Minneapolis: Augsburg Fortress, 2003.

Vines, Matthew. *God and the Gay Christian: The Biblical Case in Support of Same-Sex Relationships*. Colorado Springs: Convergent Books, 2014.

Wenham, G. J. *The Book of Leviticus*, New International Commentary on the Old Testament. Grand Rapids: Eerdmans, 1979.

Wenham, Gordon. *Genesis 16–50*, Word Biblical Commentary. Nashville: Thomas Nelson, 1994.

Wold, Donald J. *Out of Order: Homosexuality in the Bible and the Ancient Near East*. Grand Rapids: Baker, 1998.

Wright, David F. "Homosexuals or Prostitutes? The Meaning of ΑΡΣΕΝΟΚΟΙΤΑΙ (1 Cor. 6:9, 1 Tim. 1:10)." *Vigiliae Christianae* 38, no. 2 (June 1984): 125–53.

Zehnder, Markus. "Observations on the Relationship between David and Jonathan and the Debate on Homosexuality." *Westminster Theological Journal* 69, no. 1 (Spring 2007): 127–74.